Backpackers & Flashpackers

in Western Europe:
500 Hostels in 100 Cities in 25 Countries

Hardie Karges

ISBN: 0988490501

ISBN 13: 978-0988490505

Library of Congress Control Number: 2012919932

Hypertravel Books, Los Angeles, CA

Table of Contents

Preface: Me And My Big Idea

It's not often that REALLY BIG THINGS happen in any field of life, love, or endeavor, much less accommodations, and budget ones, at that. So it was with some surprise and wonder, that I looked out the window of the Bangkok Skytrain high above Sukhumwit Road a few years back and saw a hostel, the word emblazoned like a flag to the weary on the edge of one of the world's largest red-light districts. I remember thinking, "WTF?" (I didn't know text-talk back then, so I thought the actual words). I used to live in Thailand by the way, but not Bangkok. I'd been in a "youth hostel" or two before, also, but wasn't too impressed with the institutional atmosphere or the customary curfews, as if I were a school-boy who needed to be tucked in at night. And what was one doing a few short blocks from Soi Cowboy, which was known for neither, institutionality or curfews, and whose cowboys may spend time in the saddle, but hardly of horses? In short: they're not just for schoolboys any more.

Hostels are the biggest thing to happen in the field of accommodation since B&B's came on the scene a half-century ago, an extension of that concept, almost, in that both are a non-traditional-hotel option. But whereas B&B's have gone up-market, and were never particularly cheap in the first place (not in America at least), hostels are largely defined by their budget orientation. The big change is that they're no longer defined by their institutional nature, or their curfews, or even the youth of their customers. These days most hostels are as individualistic as any B&B ever was, and the individuals using them are extremely diverse in nationality, occupation, and age. There are inner-city hostels, suburban hostels, country hostels, funky hostels, high-style hostels, art hostels, and most of all—party hostels. And there are still youth hostels, of course. That's one reason this guide exists, in fact, to create some order out of a very desirable, but sometimes chaotic, situation.

So I'm using all the information at my disposal to ultimately try to put it all in book form, starting with Europe, the motivating principle to be as comprehensive and accurate as possible in explaining and cataloging hostels. My underlying and ultimate goal, though, is to re-inject some spontaneity into backpacking, which is one of its greatest turn-ons for me. As it is, hostels typically require much advance online booking and planning to make it work smoothly. That means you'll be committed to a schedule, though, more or less, and once it becomes all too packaged, then it's nothing more than a poor man's travel itinerary. Backpacking and world travel are better than that. If I do my job well here, then you should be able to have the best of both worlds, inexpensive and spontaneous. Hopefully you can even leave those half-dozen 500-page guidebooks at home. This is all you really need, after all, this and an Internet device. And yes, I've been to almost all of these countries, all but one in fact, and I recommend them all.

I've traveled for almost forty years now, mostly backpacker-style, in some 145 countries, so I've certainly seen many changes over the years, and not all for the good. Cities are larger and more crowded now, for the most part. And many of those little fishing villages that once seemed so perfect—cheap, beautiful, authentic and pristine—are now themselves overcrowded and overpriced tourist resorts. Too often the paradise I once found is now paradise lost. Simply winging it "footloose," wandering from town to town with little advance planning, is especially problematic now, as I found out myself not long ago when I arrived in London on a Saturday night without a hotel reservation. Ouch! But one thing that **has** changed for the better is the virtual explosion of hostels over the last decade. I'm tempted to call it a movement, though that may be overstating the case; but not by much. See you in Bilbao.

Introduction

What is a hostel? Originally they were places, mostly in Europe, where students could sleep for cheap on extended country outings, frequently established at appropriate intervals over and about the landscape and which corresponded more or less to the amount of distance a student might hike or bike in the course of a day. Since those outings usually occurred in the summer when schools were otherwise uncommitted, the schools themselves became the logical place for seasonal conversion. That still happens sometimes, but not much. The concept has expanded dramatically over the last decade, for a variety of reasons, no doubt; among them: rising hotel prices, rising restaurant prices, and—drum roll here, please—Internet. For the rise of Internet has not only made advance booking widely accessible for both hostel and traveler, but it also became a reasonably-priced accommodation where a traveler would almost certainly have access to that same Internet. This fueled an explosion which is still happening to this day, and has barely scratched the surface yet in many places.

In the introduction to my book "Hypertravel: 100 Countries in 2 Years," I wrote, "Not surprisingly, hostels are least prevalent in places where cheap hotels and guest houses are most available, such as Southeast Asia." I just might have to return the Cuban cigar I received for that brilliant observation. At last count Singapore had over forty hostels, and even very-reasonably-priced Bangkok almost as many. In contrast Boston, in the good ol' US of A, has… what, two or three? I guess hostels, with their shared rooms, just aren't American. But all that's changing, especially in New York, with some of the highest hotel rates in the world. Even in Africa, especially southern Africa, the concept is huge and growing, and in Latin America, they're fairly abundant. The only problem is that there exists something of a flexible and locally-influenced definition of what really makes a good hostel, so that this guide to European hostels will reflect those considerations.

What any good hostel should have, by my own current standards, are: 1) cheap dorm beds, 2) English language, 3) a kitchen, 4) storage lockers, and 5) easy access to Internet. Of course within each of those categories there exists significant margin for deviation, but a place of lodging should make the effort to at least offer something in each of these five basic requirements in my humble opinion. Other things you can expect that probably wouldn't be considered "amenities" include DIY bedding (you know how to make a bed, right?) and the likely absence of a towel (though many have it, but charge). For purposes of this guide I had to decide what ultimately defines a hostel, and for me that's the shared rooms. It's nice, for me at least, if they have private rooms also, but if they don't have dorms, then they won't be in this book. This book is not intended to be comprehensive, so don't be surprised if you don't see your favorite party hostel in Belgrade. This book tries to be selective. There's a reason for that, several of them, in fact.

There are some downsides with hostels in general, though usually no more than the sometimes institutional nature of them. A bigger problem can be location, especially where they're rare. That hostel may be located far from the center and not obvious even when standing right in front of it, no sign of the business conducted within, many of them no doubt informal in their business approach. There are other issues, also, such as the once-standard curfews which are rapidly disappearing. Then there are the also-once-standard age limits, also in decline, though still there, the main problem being one of where to draw the line. I've seen upper limits anywhere between thirty-five and fifty-five. That's problematic for those of us who hold non-discrimination dearly *and who are already over fifty-five*.

Other hostels are more creative and limit ages only within dorm rooms. That sounds reasonable, especially given the other discrimination issue: most dorms are of mixed sexes, though female-only dorms are not uncommon. It's mostly cool and without problems, but still these are valid issues to consider. Most backpackers' hostels simply have no age limit, and that's the way it should be, I feel. Any problems can be dealt with on an individual basis. Another related problem is that in some cities of Europe hostel beds rank as decent long-term accommodations for some individuals and even families, who attempt to live there. Most hostels rightfully attempt to discourage this, as they should. Hostels are not transient hotels, after all. I try to weed those places out.

It gets worse. Some small hostels are barely staffed, if at all, absentee landlords showing up to let you in and set you up, then disappearing until the next guest shows up. Many legitimate "boutique" hotels do that, too, especially in northern Europe, where they rightfully value their own private lives, but others are merely renting a flat and calling it a hostel, with little regard to your needs or that of their neighbors. If you book in advance, and they demand to know your arrival time, then that's a good clue. If they call you in advance, that's another. If they have no website and the hostel-booking site has few pictures, then that's another. Unfortunately a place with a bad rep can simply change its name and start all over as if nothing ever happened. I try to weed those places out of this guide and include only "real" hostels. With this guide you can contact hostels directly before committing any money, which is good. That way you can do some weeding, too, even at the last minute. You can't do that with most hostel-booking sites, which for many hostels is their only connection to potential customers.

For better or worse, consolidation is setting in to the hostel scene rapidly, and the days of the "hippie hostel" may be numbered. The most obvious manifestation of this trend is the appearance of hostel chains, not only within a city or country, but in multiple cities across a region, especially Western Europe. I think that this in general is good, as it establishes standards of services and expectations. The downside, that quirky little mom-and-pop operations may get squeezed out, is probably misplaced, since many of those places wouldn't rate very highly on my hostel-meter anyway, and the current "Air BnB" trend is probably more suitable to their offerings. Many of those would not even be found in this book, since they don't have websites. Conversely, many of the biggest chains will not be represented for every one of their branches here. I try to strike a balance between standards and individuality. Just because a place calls itself a hostel is not enough for me.

A word should be mentioned about HI, Hostelling International, which is often affiliated with YHA and such. This is the original hostel chain, and largely responsible for the existence of hostels, or at least their smooth transition from those early schoolboy barracks into modern backpackers' party hostels. They are a membership organization and you will need to pay an extra charge to stay there if youre not a member. When you've done this a half-dozen times or so, you'll be a member. But this guide is not about HI, though some are listed, particularly the ones that offer beds on the major hostel-booking sites. In fact they could probably fill a book larger than this of only their member hostels worldwide, though many of their branches are open only seasonally, so I won't concentrate much on them. For better or worse, they tend to represent the old school of "youth hostels" more than the modern era of "backpackers."

By the way in some quarters a hostel itself is known as a "backpackers," short for "backpackers' hostel," I assume. Make a note. Also, pricing gets elaborate and confusing, and frequently changing, so are included here for comparison purposes only. Just know that in Western Europe a dorm bed will likely run $20-50 and in Eastern Europe somewhat less, maybe as little as half that. And for a private room, you'll have to pay that same price for two to three people, regardless of how many actually occupy the room. You should be aware that in some places—London comes to mind—you might do better price-wise for a small cramped private room in one of the chock-a-block centers of budget accommodation around Earl's Court, Victoria Coach Station, or Shepherd's Bush. That's when some of the other considerations come in, like Wi-Fi or a kitchen or…

The best thing about a hostel I've hardly even mentioned yet, because it's a hard thing to quantify, and that's the people you'll meet. Even an old geezer like me needs some social intercourse (yep) from time to time, and given our frequent differences from the locals, travelers are the next best thing. In out-of-the-way places like Armenia or Namibia, that's priceless. In places like London, that's "Party Time!" Don't forget to wear protection (for your ears, that is). So that's pretty much what hostels aka "backpackers" are all about. But what's a "flashpacker," you ask? I think that's what you become when you've been a backpacker too long and can't stop, maybe a little older, hopefully a little wiser, more up-scale and maybe less group-oriented, i.e. hardcore, or maybe 'die-hard.' I guess that's me. Some flashpackers may also be more urban and less interested in remote locations than in partying in the pubs. That's not me.

If you're American, then you're probably wondering why this historic trend seems to have skipped over the good ol' USA. Actually it didn't, really. Ever heard of the YMCA? They're always booked up in New York. This book's for you. America's indeed the last to get in on the modern trend, but I expect that to change very soon. I think many Americans just can't see themselves staying in dorms, but that's half the fun if you're young, and a surefire way to meet people. So what makes this book better than a website for booking hostels? That's like comparing apples and oranges. For one thing, we give you the hostel's own website and/or e-mail address and phone number for direct communication. So, not only can we be more objective than a booking site that receives a commission, but a booking site may show a hostel to be full when a call or e-mail to the hostel itself will get you a bed immediately. For another, we try to include only the "real" hostels, hopefully without bad reviews. But if they don't have dorms, then they won't be here, and likely the same result if they have no website.

This is intended as an introduction and complement to the vast online resources and hopefully a broader view. Still, hostel-booking sites are invaluable for feedback, specific information and special promotions, and I urge everyone to consult them. Two of the bigger ones that I know best are *www.hostelbookers.com* and *www.hostelworld.com*, though there are many others, and *www.hostelz.com* acts as something of a "kayak" for them all, so that's good. Then there's the membership-only *www.hihostels.com*, but as mentioned before, that's more likely an old-school "youth hostel," so not really the focus here, though some are included and I'd say almost all are "real" by my definition. If you're looking for something out in the countryside, they may even be best. But we're getting ahead of ourselves. This is a travel guide (both time and space) as well as a hostel guide. If you're a novice traveler, then you need to know some basics first.

Travel Basics & Traveling Around Western Europe

Transportation: Buses, Trains, & Planes

There's nothing more basic to travel than the actual transportation. In general that means buses, trains, and planes, right? Well, for international travel, especially inter-continental travel, that mostly means planes. But which planes? Well, you can just go to a travel agent and they'll be happy to do everything for you, but if you're a do-it-yourselfer like me, then you probably want a little bit more control over the process than that, and you probably wouldn't mind knowing how it works, so that you can tweak it to your own tastes and proclivities. The good news is that with online booking you can do that. I do things in the booking process I wouldn't dare ask an agent to do. The first thing to decide is where and when you want to go, and then start pricing.

First determine what's the nearest major hub city (usually the largest and the lowest price) in the region you're going to, or coming from, and then compare to that. Major hubs around the world include London, Paris, Cairo, Istanbul, Dubai, Johannesburg, Delhi, Bangkok, Singapore, Lima, and others. In the US: New York, LA, San Francisco, Chicago, Miami, Houston, Dallas and Atlanta are the biggies, in no certain order. If you're traveling abroad and want a multi-city route, then carefully check for airlines that hub in one of the cities on your route, for instance for LA-Paris-Cairo-LA, you'll definitely want to check Egyptair and Air France, in addition to a multi-line site or two. Expedia and the like can and will book any multi-segment flight on multiple airlines, very convenient!

Are you still with me? So what's next? In the old days I'd check the Sunday travel section in LA, New York, or San Fran papers—the library'd have them if the newsstands didn't—and start looking for deals from "bucket shops," i.e. consolidators. They'd buy large blocks of seats to re-sell and always undercut the airlines themselves, who were limited by IATA rules and regs in what they could do. Then I'd get on the 800# line and start chatting with someone with a thick accent in Times Square or Union Square or Chinatown or on Broadway downtown somewhere, trying to get the right price. It'd never be the price in the ad, of course, but I'd try to get close. Then I'd make payment and ticketing arrangements to be mailed back and forth, money order for them, paper ticket usually Fedexed to me, very "old school." Or if I were stopping in that same city on my way out of the country, then I might even stop in their office, if I could squeeze into the cramped spaces they typically occupied. Those ads have mostly disappeared.

It's easier than that now. Some of those places still exist—Flight Center and STA Travel come to mind as multi-city biggies—but rarely will they have better deals now than what you could find for yourself on the Net. I usually go to one of the major multi-airline travel sites like Expedia, CheapoAir, etc. (or Kayak will pull them all up for you to compare) and see who flies where and when for how much. Then I'll go to the website of one or more of those airlines and compare prices. They're not always the same, and as often as not the multi-airline site will be cheaper, BUT… that might change tomorrow. The airline's own site will change less, but the multi-line sites can somehow magically splice together several airlines for multi-city itineraries, all at very reasonable prices. They also have hotels, too, but if you're reading this book, then that's probably not your thing. One advantage to Expedia, etc. is that prices include tax; with airlines' own sites, you'll probably have to continue to checkout. Don't be fooled by false low numbers.

When to buy? You know that already, don't you? The sooner you buy, the better the price, right? Not necessarily. Of course you need to check as far in advance as possible just to budget yourself, but I'd say start checking prices seriously no later than three months before your anticipated travel date. But don't buy yet. Online sales are usually immediate, so you probably want to keep options open as long as you can. A travel agent might make a reservation for you and let you pay later, so that's one advantage to working with them. Then if you find it cheaper yourself, you can cancel with the agent or simply let it expire. Don't book the same flight as the one your agent's already booked, though. That gets messy.

I'd still advise you to do some legwork, regardless. If your dates are flexible, then check prices for each day a week before and after your preferred date; they'll probably vary, but Tuesday and Wednesday will usually be cheapest. Check again a week later; it goes fast when you get the hang of it. If prices start going up for Fridays then you might want to go ahead and purchase that Wednesday flight. If not, then wait. I've seen some major discounts right at two months out, if the seats aren't selling quickly enough, so wait until then if you can, fifty-nine days out if your plans are firm enough. If not then start monitoring every day or two. A large group can sell a flight out quickly. Once a seat is gone, they rarely come back. It's not like the old days when reservations were made, then frequently cancelled.

If you're trying to book a frequent-flyer flight from an airline, generally a tiered system will charge you a certain amount of miles for Europe (50K+/-), Asia (75K+/-), Africa (100K+/-), etc. without any advantage necessarily to the major hubs. Those hubs may have stiffer fees and taxes, too, and the award usually doesn't cover that. I'm searching flights to Africa from the US right now, hubbing out of Europe. It costs 40,000 frequent-flyer miles to fly to either London or Lisbon. London's fees are $600; Lisbon's are $200. Go figure. If you're using frequent-flyer miles attached to a major non-airline bank card, then usually now those convert to 1% of the cost of the flight, i.e. 50,000 miles = $500 flight, booking through their agent. Poke around the site first, though, and you might find a minor partner that still uses the old tier system (like Bank of America's Canadian partner). You'll likely get more that way if you're flexible with dates. Whew!

To go to West Europe check the multi-airline flight booking sites and see if there are any deals to the big European hubs, then check nearby dates and times and places to compare. Then check the airlines' own site(s) to compare. If you're going from America, and traveling all over Europe, then London is probably your best bet, or Paris if the Continent is your focus, maybe Amsterdam. The Europe-American flights are handled by all major American airlines plus British Air, Air France, Lufthansa, KLM, Airitalia, Virgin, Iberia, and others, but sometimes the Asian/Pacific carriers might be cheaper, like Air New Zealand or Singapore Air. Flying from the east coast opens up other possibilities, like Icelandic Air, which allows a three-day stopover in Reykjavik at no extra charge. You heard it here, remember, lucky you.

Once you get into Europe, you already know what to do, right? Get a Eurail Pass, right? Sucker... Things are really good for flying around now, arguably a "movement" as important as that of hostelling—the explosion of budget airlines in Europe over the last decade. The originals EasyJet and RyanAir are still two of the best. There are literally hundreds, so choose carefully and google hard. You won't find these flights with agents or on multi-airline booking sites. Many major airlines are also forming budget subsidiaries for regional flights, too. Note that many budget airlines go to out-of-the-way suburban airports, so not always convenient. Buses usually connect to the nearest city center.

Buses are still a good option for getting from country to country, but not necessarily within countries. The Western European heartland—France, Germany, Italy, etc.—is so train-centric that bus systems are not well-developed, except at the extreme local level, feeding customers to the ubiquitous trains. Between countries Eurolines and their partners dominate. They tend to be friendly to backpackers, since real (upscale) travelers ride on trains or planes. They're reasonably priced, and go places that planes don't. Terminals are usually located in city centers, and they'll use ferry crossings wherever that applies. West European countries that have well-developed bus systems of their own include Ireland, the UK, Spain, and Scandinavia. For example, buses from London go all over, including Northern Ireland, via ferries, and Europe, too. They're cheaper than trains, even if a little less convenient. There are both to Europe, via the Chunnel, though budget airlines have stolen much of that thunder.

So what of the ubiquitous trains and their special Eurail Passes designed-just-for-us-tourists-so-don't-even-try-to-get-one-there? I love trains, and they're very convenient, so that's reason enough to ride them, at least some of the time. I've only bought one Eurail Pass in my life, but I figure they're a rip-off. They're not for sale there, because no one would buy them, and people would advise their American friends the same (if they didn't die laughing first). You'd have to travel non-stop to get your money's worth on a Eurail Pass if my previous calculations still hold true. The problem is that there are all these fees and surcharges that the Pass doesn't cover, so it's neither cheap nor convenient. Of course I quickly realized there were ways to easily cheat the two-week multi-country one I had where you fill in the dates, but that would be wrong.

Visas: Consulates, Passports, & Letters of Introduction

Depending on your nationality and where you're going, you might need a visa, which is a stamp in your passport that is your permit to enter a specific country. They have to be applied for at an embassy or a consulate. Do that two to three months before travel, also, if possible. You already knew you needed a passport, right? Don't worry; it can usually all be done by mail, but allow plenty of time, and make sure your passport has at least six months of validity from the date you plan to enter the last country on your itinerary or they might not let you in. Visas can sometimes be picked up on the road, but get as many as you can in advance from your home, especially if you live in a major city that has embassies and consulates. Nothing is certain out there. There are companies that will do it for you, but it can get quite expensive. Google hard, but the best source for knowing what visas you'll need (if you're American) is probably *http://travel.state.gov*. Other countries have their own. If you're doing the work yourself, then check the websites of the countries whose visa you need to get instructions.

If you're an American going to Western Europe, there are no visas required, same for citizens of most other "developed" (read: "rich") countries. You travelers from developing countries might need some, better check with individual countries' websites to be sure. As parties to the Schengen Agreement, the rules for one country in Europe should be the same for all of them (except Ireland and the UK).

Money: Currencies, Exchange Rates, and ATM's

Money is important when traveling, of course, the more the better, but you don't have to actually carry it all with you. In general I recommend ATM's, since traveler's checks are almost extinct, and you usually have to find a bank to cash them, as opposed to the generally more available exchange booths. The problem with ATM's is that they aren't everywhere in the world, believe it or not, and service charges can be high. If you plan to travel a lot, it's worth getting a bank account that doesn't charge much for foreign transactions. You need cash, too, of course, and a credit card for emergencies, so I recommend a mix of them all, a few traveler's checks, too, if you've got them. You don't want to get stuck with extra foreign currency, though Euros or Pounds are not so bad since easily changeable almost everywhere. There's an art to using up your worthless currency. Buy gifts at the end of a trip to use up extra currency. The last few days change just what you need until you cross the next border.

Change money at established locations unless you're desperate, and count your money carefully whether at an exchange house, at a bank, or on the street. But first look at the posted rates, both of them. There's a "buying" rate and a "selling" rate. Unless you're leaving the country and want dollars or Euros or whatever back, then the buying rate is the one you're getting, the lower of the two. If it's a good rate, then there should be no more than 2-3% difference between the two. If it's more than five I'd probably pass, unless I'm desperate. Also check to see if there are commissions or extra charges. In Western Europe there usually are. Use ATM's. Use any leftover currency immediately at the border or first stop of the new country you're entering, or you might be stuck with it. Some currencies are non-convertible, e.g. Belarusian rubles. Use 'em up. Never exchange money at a US airport on the way out. It's a rip-off, same in West Europe. If I need to carry cash in US Dollars, then I usually prefer fifty-dollar-bills, since they'll get as good of a rate as hundreds, are usually prettier, and are easier to cash in a pinch. Old worn bills won't pass.

Euro is the most widely used currency in Western Europe, of course, but there are others, too. English pounds (aka quid, sterling) are used all over the UK, but the reverse is not always true. Don't use an ATM in Scotland unless you have to; and even then, use it well before all your English pounds have run out. You'll get Scottish pounds, maybe hard to pass down south. You've been warned. The Republic of Ireland is a different political entity entirely and uses the Euro. It is accessible overland from Northern Ireland and by ferry from England, ditto the Isle of Man, which is a self-governing crown colony, and Manx pounds are used there in addition to sterling. Except for Finland all Scandinavian countries plus Switzerland, still have their own currencies. Greece is not sure.

Communications: Cell-phones, Phone Cards & Computers

I think this is where the phrase, "it's complicated," originates. If you're European or from most anywhere else in the world besides the US, then it's easier. But America is slow to get on the worldwide GSM digital network standard for cell phones, and that's what you need, that and a multi-band phone, one that can handle both 1900 (Am) and 1800 (rest of world) band frequencies. Most new phones will make the switch automatically; if not, then look in the menu for something like settings>network>band, and then choose the one you need. If you're already with AT&T, T-Mobile or another GSM network in the US, then your phone should work all around the world, albeit with high international roaming charges. You may need to activate world service first. Poke around the website, though, and you might find some special arrangements for particular countries. Barring that, if you're going to be in any one country for very long, then it's worth buying a local SIM card and putting it in your phone.

What's a SIM card? Simply put: that little thumbnail-size circuit-board accessible through the back of the phone is your number and all the information that goes with it, including your calling history. It's easy to switch, but you'll probably have to "unlock" your phone first if it's American. American cell-phone services are traditionally monopolized, with prices to match. If that's what it takes to produce iPhones, then so be it. If you're switching services in the US, then request the company to unlock it. If you're tech-savvy, you might even find tools online to unlock it yourself. Otherwise, go to the sleazy part of town in some sleazy city (say, London) where people do things they're not supposed to do and look for signs around cell-phone shops that say "phones unlocked," or something like that. Buy a local SIM card for ten or fifteen bucks, stick it in, and then start blabbing. Some might even be worth keeping, if they give you a better international rate than your US phone would.

Smart phones are too new for me to have the skinny worldwide. G4 phones may make the preceding information obsolete, but I can't guarantee it yet. Buy the next edition, and I'll promise to be up-to-date by then. This is a real breakthrough, obviously, to have a local map in your hands constantly and ready to use. It's not that easy, though, not yet anyway. For one thing, there are the high roaming fees mentioned earlier. For another, the G3 system doesn't exist everywhere in the world yet, much less G4, so simply buying a new SIM card and sticking it in is not necessarily a quick easy solution. Stay tuned. As a lover of maps, I find this development exciting if only for that reason. After all, who do I want to call in most countries that I travel in? But maps are something else entirely.

Actually phone-cards are still popular and useful, but you don't always need actual cards. Sometimes all you need are the PIN number and the access numbers, so you can do that online with much greater choice than in Chinatown. Ones that allow you to call all over the world from the US are dirt cheap. Ones that allow calling from anywhere to everywhere might be harder to find and more expensive. Read the fine print carefully. Of course even then you'll need a local phone to call the access number, so maybe not worth the hassle for a traveler.

The more modern alternative is to use Skype on your Internet device: anywhere everywhere cheap no hassle, all you need is WiFi for calling out or even receiving calls whenever you happen to be online. For someone to call you anywhere any time, though, you still need your own number. Skype rates may finally be climbing now, but there are copycats with similar services to compare to. As for Internet in general, Wi-Fi is an international standard, so available everywhere, of course, but don't expect them to be everywhere for free. Since you're reading this book, though, your odds are very good with the places listed here. One nice thing about G-4 cell-phone-style Internet is that it'll be everywhere there's phone service and quality should be comparable to WiFi. Then those GSM (GPRS) modems that connect to the USB port of your Internet device should truly be competitive with ADSL high-speed Internet. As with cell-phones if you're going to be around a while, it might be worth it to buy a local SIM for your GSM modem.

Security: Rip-offs, Scams and Insurance

Of course you need to be careful at all times when traveling. You're especially vulnerable when walking around with a full pack. Don't waste time in that situation; don't do it after dark; and don't even think about it in Jo'burg, or anywhere in South Africa, for that matter. And spread that money around, on your body, that is. Don't keep everything in one easy place. Losing a little is much better than losing a lot. Got a passport bag? Don't dangle it off your neck, either inside or out. Put your arm through it and conceal it snugly under your armpit, ready to be locked down tightly, with your arm. Carry that daypack in front or off your side; a thief in a group following you closely behind can riddle through your bag without you even knowing it. Be careful with strangers; maintain some distance. If anyone gets too close, or follows behind for too long, then stop! Let him pass.

Put that wallet in your front pocket; butts aren't so sensitive usually. Avoid crowds in general; but if you're in a crowd and feel a bump, then grab your bag or wallet immediately. You might feel someone else's hand there. That's how pickpockets work. Don't confront them; they're fast. You won't even be sure who it was. Tight passages are the same. Pickpockets wait there to pass through at the same time as you. Deal is: when you feel the bump, you won't feel the grab. If you're walking around after dark, consider carrying something gnarly in your hand, like an umbrella or a flashlight or a nasty-looking set of keys. A belt with heavy buckle that slides right out of the loops fast works well. Most thieves want to work quickly, but not all. There are slow scams and false fawning fraudulent friends, too. Remember to wear protection.

This is all for deterrence, remember; you never want to ever actually get into a tangle. If someone acts menacingly toward you and they're not yet close, then run like Hell. If they pull a gun or knife, then give them whatever they want. Your life is worth more than your iPad. In the unfortunate event that you do get robbed or mugged, don't panic. Go to the police, get a report, and start the work of canceling credit cards and getting a new passport. That means going to the nearest consulate or embassy and telling them you need an emergency termporary passport. They can usually do it in a few hours. If they imply otherwise, then talk to someone else. It can be done; I've done it. Hopefully you've got a copy of the passport; that helps. A birth certificate also helps. Remember to allow extra time at the airport of your departure, as they'll need to fix the entry stamp that's now in your lost passport. Hopefully you've got a few bucks stashed away. That helps. Don't be shy about asking for help. Get religion; that helps.

Political security is another consideration, and for an American the most thorough update is from the site already mentioned: http://travel.state.gov, then divide by half and that's about right (they're more cautious than your mama). Keeping up with the news is a good idea, especially for the countries where you're going. Last decade's war zones can be great travel bargains, though, like Belfast, Belgrade, Beirut, and... give Baghdad some more time.

Simply put: be careful and don't take chances. An ounce of prevention is worth a kilo of cure.

I'm not a big insurance guy, considering it in general to be a rip-off, but others have differing opinions. If you're booking a flight on a multi-line booking site, it'll be available there, sometimes on individual airlines' websites also. Some promote it heavily to pad the bill; you might have to opt out to get it off the bill. If you're going somewhere dangerous, that ups the ante a bit, of course.

Some European countries are starting to require insurance to enter their country, or so they say, but no word yet on how that's being enforced. I've never bought any kind of insurance for Europe. Western Europe has few specific security situations of an epidemic or endemic political nature, probably the safest place in the world, actually.

Health: Vaccinations, Food and Drugs

You know the drill, right? Multiple rounds of shots wherever you go and for the tropics, don't forget the prophylaxis, right? To be honest, I've never gotten most of those shots, just the ones required by law, but it would be irresponsible of me to suggest that you do the same. Tropical areas are certainly the problem, so require extra caution, though yellow fever is usually the only shot actually required by law. If you have to get that in the US just to get a visa, then it'll set you back a cool $100-150. If you can get it on the road somewhere, then it might be as little as ten bucks. Ask at public health centers; sometimes they'll jab you right at the border, just to facilitate matters. Some vaccines seem not much better than the disease, so use your judgment. Malaria prophylaxis is easy enough if you're actually entering a malarial area, but so are mosquito nets. Don't ever have sex with locals without a condom.

If the food seems strange at first wherever you happen to be, then go slow with it, allow your bacteria some time to adapt. You should experiment, though, since some of the local delicacies are delicious. Just make sure that foods have been recently made and are best served hot. The nose knows. Ask locally about water quality, though it's usually easy enough to drink bottled water or boil tap water first to be sure.

As for recreational drugs, I've got a simple rule: nothing never no way no how; just kidding! But you should be aware of the risks. A lot of countries take simple possession of marijuana as a *very serious offense*, punishable by death, or you might wish you're dead by the end of it. I would not advise traveling with ganja anywhere in the world. That smell is hard to get out. If you just gotta' have a little smoke once in a while, then I advise you to befriend the hipsters wherever you end up, which carries its own set of risks. Better yet, why not just quit for a while? You might be amazed how much easier you catch that buzz when you get home. It's the contrast that counts. Being stoned all the time is no fun. Of course more and more countries are legalizing it, so that's good. Latin America may soon be a dope-friendly continent, what with Uruguay already legal and others considering it, most of them tolerant, Europe too. Asia is intolerant.

Unfortunately more and more Muslim countries are outlawing alcohol, so it's the same thing. Take a break; you'll enjoy it more if/when you start back. Many Muslim-lite countries are growing more fundamentalist. Your best bet there are hotels, which are often considered international zones exempt from local standards. Remember that wherever you are, especially poor countries, that as a rich (yes) foreigner, you're vulnerable, so be careful. If you've just got to get a buzz once in a while, you might consider checking out the pharmacies. Things are legal overseas that are controlled tightly in the US; be creative, and read instructions carefully. It might be a good time to fix that cough. The cough syrup overseas is excellent. Check the ingredients. It even cures coughs… sometimes.

If you've got a serious drug habit, then you really should de-tox. It doesn't go well with travel. You should be careful even when drinking with locals. Mickeys do get slipped, and so do roofies. Finish that drink before going to the head. Don't accept drinks already opened, in bars or buses or trains, whether alcohol, milk or water. It's better to offend than to get robbed. Let me be clear that I do not advocate any drug use myself (I rarely if ever even drink now) but I understand the desire, so wish to see it done responsibly. But if you think you'll stay in hostels because those sound like cool places to smoke pot, then think again. I've never—I repeat, **never**—seen so much as a joint smoked at a hostel. Alcohol, yes, that's fairly common in hostels, but not pot.

West Europe has its own set of concerns. Many people go to Amsterdam for recreational cannabis use, of course, though it is scheduled to be curtailed for foreigners. That's a shame, since it really is a pretty cool scene. But if it's causing crime, then that's a problem. It doesn't help that some tourists flaunt it, toking up in McDonald's just to prove they can. Things may not truly change until it's legal everywhere, removing the need for specialized tourism. Portugal has an official policy of tolerance now, but you are advised not to buy from sleazeballs on the street. Ask around, I guess, if you're going to be there for a while. Western Europe is the healthiest place in the world, and medical care might even be thrown in for free. Don't try that in the US.

Cultural Considerations: Sex, Religion and Politics

Among Western or westernized countries it's no big deal, of course. Our informality is our calling card and our stock in trade. That's not true elsewhere, though it's tricky to intuit. Some of the rockingest whoringest countries can be quite conservative amongst locals, Thailand for instance. In Thailand you'll rarely see locals kissing in public, though in the international zone, you'll see much more than that, of course. Vietnam has no such taboo, and couples hang all over each other in parks. Act conservatively until you know the local mores. As corny as it sounds, we are ambassadors to the world, and I'd like to think we have a larger mission to bring people together through our highest common denominators.

Think hard before taking on a local girlfriend, a good girl, that is. It'll take some time and patience. Women won't have such a problem, but just be warned that many local guys will only want a quick fling with a wild Western woman. If and when it comes time to do the nasty, always keep a few millimeters between you and the object of your affection. Anything else would be the ultimate in foolishness. Politics is always a bit dicey to discuss in public unless you know your host and his or her inclinations. Some places there can even be legal repercussions, such as Communist countries and a few Muslim ones. Tone it down. Most cultural considerations usually boil down to something much more mundane, though. Shoes are customarily removed when entering houses, and sometimes buildings, in much of the world, whether Buddhist, Hindu, or Muslim, so please comply willingly. They take it seriously.

Most travelers are Western European by ethnicity if not nationality, or are Westernized Asians, so travel there is no big surprise, even for Americans. But Americans would do well to tone down loud rude behavior. Europeans tend to be a bit more quiet and introspective. The "ugly American" is an image that still grates on nerves there. In Amsterdam coffeehouses, smokers do not pass joints, either; sorry, bro. Most of Western Europe has largely followed America's lead in curtailing tobacco smoking. That's good news.

What to Pack: Clothes, Communications and Cosmetics

There's one simple rule: travel light. I personally carry a day-pack and a laptop computer bag **only,** no matter the destination, no matter the length of the trip. Forget the monopoly board; forget the five-pound toilet kit; and most of all: **forget the library** (including all those 500-page travel guides), except for this book, of course. A laptop or Nook or Kindle can hold all the books you'll ever need *or you can buy whatever you need whenever you need it.* That is true of almost everything. A few changes of clothing are all you need, and a change of shoes, preferably a variety of things that can be layered as needed. The trick is to wash clothes as you go along, every chance you get, very easy if you have a private room with sink, not so easy in a dorm, but they frequently have machines there, so do everything up whenever you get the chance, except the set you're wearing.

Wear those hiking boots when you actually travel, so you never have to pack them. Add a pair of flipflops or kung fu slippers or sneakers to that, and you're set. My secret item is a down padded vest, which will compress to almost nothing, and keep you very warm in the coldest situations (plus cushion your pack and be a bus pillow and…). Add a long-sleeve shirt, and a T-shirt or two, which can go under or alone, a couple flowery shirts to accompany those pheromones you'll be sending to the opposite sex, a pair of long pants, a pair of shorts and a pair for swimming, and you're set. Use small 100ml bottles for toiletries (per carry-on restrictions), a needle and thread, a small umbrella, a power adaptor for multiple countries (and dorm rooms with few sockets), a luggage lock, and… That's about it. Don't forget the Internet device.

Western Europe has no specific requirements except what might be dictated by weather: beach or mountains, summer or winter, rainy or dry. European electric plugs are usually the round two-prong type, so you'll need an adaptor for that. UK has a big-ass three-prong plug, though. Power is 220-240 volts, not the 110 common to the US, but most portable appliances—cell-phones, laptops, etc. seem to be able to handle both. Check the label to be sure.

Travel Guides: Books, Maps and Internet

Guidebooks and Internet should work together for travel, but I think the relative importance is reversed. Instead of carrying a big book around for your basic travel information and then using Internet to book hostels and play around on FaceBook, I suggest using Internet for basic travel information, too. Not only is the amount of information enormous, but it's updated constantly. This book can help finding hostels, too, whether you have Internet or not. For me large travel guides are not only an anachronism, but were never really necessary in the first place, maybe to read up on beforehand, but not to travel with. I've rarely traveled with one. Most travel is largely intuitive, and a book removes you from that. I would recommend it only in the most remote or linguistically-challenging places, when it might really aid survival.

One thing I DO like to travel with are maps. But they're cumbersome, hard to find and harder to handle. Once again Internet is perfect for this, every place in the world available from multiple views. The Internet links I've provided here all contain maps within their sites, though a simple Google search is easy enough. I look at maps the way some people look at pornography; I can't get enough of them. One of the main problems with hostels, of course, is that they're hard to find, so that you almost need detailed destructions at some point regardless. I'm hoping that this guide can help bring hostels into the mainstream and promote some standardization. There will always be local and regional quirks as to how they operate.

How Hostels Work

But for a few small differences, a hostel works the same as any hotel, guesthouse, lodge, B&B, whatever. I won't insult your intelligence by explaining to you that basically you're paying for a place to sleep. Where it differs mostly from the others is that at a hostel you'll likely be sharing your room with a bunch of others in similar bunk beds. That creates a unique set of circumstances which requires some attention to detail. First there's the booking process. If you're staying in a dorm, then often you'll have to decide how many roommates you want. The more roommates you have, the less the price generally.

Hostels are generally booked in advance; otherwise they can be hard to find. That's once reason this book exists, to help with last-minute walk-ups and walk-ins. That's very possible in much of Europe where hostels are properly signed and conveniently located. Call first if it's a long walk or ride. I never made an advance room reservation in twenty-five years. It's nice to be spontaneous. This way you can look at it first, too, never a bad idea if you've got the time. Don't do that around midnight. Advance booking might still be cheaper, and hostel-booking sites may be cheaper than the hostel's own website. Shop and compare. If you book in advance you'll probably need to pay a deposit in advance by credit or debit card, usually 10%. Upon arrival, you'll need to pay the rest. I'll try to tell you here which take plastic, but don't count on it. Carry enough cash, just in case. If you want extra days, advise in advance if possible. For a long stay, you might want to book two or three places two or three days at the time if you don't know them well. That way, if you get a bad one, then you'll be out soon.

Obviously there is an inherent security situation with hostels that needs addressing and some malcontents seem to have figured out the basic equation faster than those in charge. I mean... I hate to be a spoilsport, here, but just because somebody stays in a hostel doesn't mean he's honest and loyal. I don't know about you, but that's my life there in that backpack, and I'm hesitant to just toss it there on the floor and walk out assuming it's secure. That's why every hostel needs lockers, and you need a lock. Lockers don't always have them, and if there are no lockers, then try to lock your pack directly to the metal frame of the bed or something similar. No thief wants to jimmy a lock if he doesn't have to; he'll take what's easiest. If you're in the room with others, don't show a lot of valuables; the walls have eyes.

Curfews are largely a thing of the past, except in the original "youth hostels," but beware the mid-day lockout, which some places impose "for cleaning," though you and I both know they're just saving on employee costs, maybe the entire profit margin at a small place. There's a good side to that, of course: the place is secure while you're out. Conversely, since the demise of the curfew, hostels have become popular places to party, sometimes facilitated by the hostel management themselves (beware in Calgary, or Tallinn, or London, or…). If the kitchen is full of liquor bottles, then that's a good sign. If there are hordes of Homies, i.e.local non-travelers, hanging out, then that's another. The yobs coming in to London from Hounslow for the weekend tend to look and act differently than the travelers from the Continent. Another sure sign is when a hostel has its own in-house bar. I'll try to tell you here when that's the case, but read the signs at check-in also.

As already mentioned, if it's a real hostel, it should have a kitchen for your use. That's nice, especially if there are no eateries nearby. Breakfast is less important, for me at least, though coffee and tea are certainly nice. So first thing I do upon arrival is stock up on food. If you wait too long, then there's no need. I tend to carry a few basics with me, so that's a start. Having a fridge is the most important thing. It's best to keep all your things in one bag and date and mark it as yours. Check the freebies bin if you're short of something. Don't take other people's food. Ask first. Most hostel people really ARE nice.

How This Book Works

How this book works is really simple. I've given you names, addresses, and phone numbers, everything but latitude and longitude, of the hostels included, so all you have to do is find the place. I advise to call ahead if you have no reservation. And I still advise booking ahead when possible, even when it's just two or three days away, so I've included website URL's, too. Many of those have contact forms within them. I've included e-mail addresses elsewhere. If you go from hostel to hostel, then you'll usually have Internet. Where this book comes in really handy is when that link is broken and you need to find a hostel when Internet is not readily available. Invariably somewhere the Internet will be down.

Of course it's the options that constitute the decision-making process in choosing a hostel, so in this guide all are listed for the following: Kitchen (or not), Breakfast (free or not or for purchase only), Wi-Fi (free or not or for purchase only), Private rooms (available or not), Lockers (available or not), and office hours. Most of this is common sense and easily understood, but a few categories may require explanation, e.g. private rooms. Hostels may be defined by their dorm beds, but for some of us, that's not optimal. I'm a light sleeper and don't appreciate being awoken in the middle of the night. Frequently I'll pay up to double to have my own room, and even then will usually come out ahead of a hotel. Nevertheless a place that has no dorms is not a hostel in my dictionary, so it's good to have both. But if you book a private room at a hostel, don't expect the same quality as a five-star hotel, or even a one-star. It's basic, but it's yours. And you might have to pay a pretty penny for that Wi-Fi elsewhere in Europe.

Lockers are fairly rare, actually, especially considering the security risk in an open dorm. Go figure. Thefts are rising. Costs are for comparison only and are something of an average, a price actually offered at a non-peak/ non-slow time of year. There are always promotions and seasonal changes and varying specifications, so check around. A hostel-booking site might be cheaper than the hostel's own site. Some hostels have free WiFi; some charge; some have none, same with computers. Contact the hostel directly if the information here is insufficient. If you don't like using a credit card online, then contact the hostel and see if other arrangements are possible. Some require full payment in advance during special seasons. There are many hostel chains now, and I may not list them all in the same town. Check their website. Most of these hostels have websites or I won't list them. Information here can be wrong. Check their website.

This book is intentionally intended to be part of a paradigm shift toward a new era in budget travel. If the old paradigm of the backpacker walking down the street with huge guidebook in hand trying to find budget accommodation is already out-of-date, then I think the one of booking them all in advance is not much better. There needs to be a balance of advance planning and spontaneity, guidebook and Internet. That's already the case, of course; I only propose to shift the balance toward less book and more Internet. This book is designed for that purpose. Not only do I hope to make hostelling better for backpackers, but I hope to see more hostels enter the mainstream, with better signage, better facilities, and ultimately more customers.

You might notice that addresses and phone numbers, everthing but Internet addresses, are listed in several different ways. That's both accidental and intentional, accidental in that I tend to leave them as they're given to me, intentional in that you'll see them many ways, so this prepares you to adapt. With phone numbers generally "+" precedes an international number. With a cell phone, hold the "0" down and "+" will appear. That saves you from having to know codes *for international calling* (011, 001, etc.) in every country. That same number used within the country would usually drop the "+" and the 2-3 number code following it and add a "0" at the front. Compare them and you'll see. A picture is worth a thousand words. Skype will add the country code for you. Now don't get all worried; go have some fun! Europe is at your fingertips!

Key to Symbols: Here are some symbols, shorthand and abbreviations used in this book:

--$> = lowest price we can find for a typical day, for comparison only (they change constantly with the season, with promotions, and with currency fluctuations)

--B'fast = Breakfast (free or not or for purchase only); typical for Europe is a "continental breakfast," pastry & drink, cereal if you're lucky; don't expect eggs; cig optional

--c.c. = credit card, OK meaning they're accepted, +/% indicating a surcharge for use; sometimes they are required as deposit, even if you're paying cash

--Desk hr = times when there should be someone to check you in. Don't press your luck.

--24/7 = they never close, supposedly. I suggest advising & confirming late arrival.

--HI, YHA, etc. = these are organizations of hostels which usually require membership; usually you can pay a small fee and gradually obtain membership

--central = hostel is centrally located in the city, generally a good thing for sight-seeing

--cash only = even if you reserved with plastic, they want cash for the balance

--luggage room, luggage OK, etc=you can stash your luggage to pick up later, very handy

--Y.H. = Youth Hostel

--lift = elevator

(note: you will also see a mini-UK flag on websites to indicate English language)

WESTERN EUROPE

Western Europe is what we usually think of as "Europe," the Germanic countries of the north and the Latin countries of the south, united by traditions of democracy and free enterprise. It's not always that easy of course—witness WWII—but the united "Eurozone" in some form or other will likely remain in existence for a long time. Its creation was something too special in the history of the world to toss away casually. For the traveler the seamless connections and predominant Euro currency within the region are like a dream come true if you've ever crossed borders elsewhere before.

Western European culture is heavily influenced by the Greeks and Romans who ruled much of the world around the time of the beginning of the Common Era. When German peoples pushed south displacing the Celts and others and impinging on the Romans, the "Pax Romana" eventually fell apart and Europe didn't return to rule the world for a thousand years, an extended "dark" time when half the people were in migration and the other half adopted feudal structures to survive. I figure at about the year 1491 the world's major cultures were all about equal—Muslim, Hindu, Buddhist, and Christian, maybe even sub-Saharan Africa and indigenous America, too. The Age of Discovery and Industrial Revolution then put the West into a dominant world position that is only now starting to show cracks.

1) Andorra

Andorra is one of those anomalies and anachronisms common to Europe, a throwback to the day when princes had 'palities (and served as buffer states between Christianity and Islam), since countries like this have little real political power. These days Andorra subsists on tourism (mostly for winter sports) and tax havens and duty-free shopping. At 181 sqare miles (468 sq km) it's still only Europe's sixth smallest. It's the only country with Catalan as chief language, and best access is from Barcelona. Spanish is widely spoken, and Euro is the currency. Telephone country code is +376.

ANDORRA LA VELLA is Andorra's capital and tourist resort *par excellence*. Once a remote rustic town, it is now a modern cosmopolitan shopper's paradise. It might be a zoo in winter, but it's right nice in summer.

www.andorra.ad/

Alberg de la Comella Hostel, Carretera de la Comella, Andorra la Vella; www.*hihostels.com,* T:+376867080, *alberglacomella@comuandorra.ad*; $24 bed>, Kitchen:N, B'fast:Y, WiFi:Y, Pvt. room:Y, Locker:Y, Desk hr:10a>8p;
Note: luggage room, lift, c.c. ok

2) Austria

The territory that is now Austria (*Osterreich*) was originally settled in the historical period by Celts, including one of Northern Europe's first high cultures at Hallstatt. After the fall of the Roman Empire, it is first documented as a German area in the *Ostarrichi* document of 996, when it was a Bavarian prefecture. Most of Austrian history, though, is about the Habsburgs, the ruling dynasty for over six hundred years, who were not only the royalty of Austria but also Holy Roman Emperors, with one exception. They accumulated land through marriage far and wide, and in those years Austria was one of the most powerful kingdoms in the world, and much more important than the land now known as Germany itself. Only the Ottoman Turks presented a real challenge and they were repulsed at the Battle of Vienna in 1683.

That all changed with the Napoleonic wars and the dissolution of the Holy Roman Empire. Germany began to unite and the question of Austria's role was paramount, it ultimately opting out. Instead the Austrian Empire of the Habsburgs joined with the Kingdom of Hungary to form Austria-Hungary, another far-flung empire of many nationalities—with some eight official languages—in an age of rising nationalism. When Archduke Franz Ferdinand (no, not the rock group) was killed by a Serb nationalist in Sarajevo, the World War was on, and the Empire was lost. WWII was no better, of course, as right-hand man to native son Hitler. So Austria has fallen a long way from its glory days, but that's probably good, since empires and monarchies are distinctive only as anachronisms of an age long gone. These days Austria, like neighbor Switzerland, is one of the wealthiest and most livable countries in the world, and life is good. The Euro is currency, German is the language, and the phone code is +43.

www.austria.info/us_b2b/

FELDKIRCH is a beautiful well-preserved medieval city, with castle, on the Austrian western border with Leichtenstein. Besides the castle, historic buildings include the Gothic parish church of Sankt Nikolaus, the town hall, and Sankt Johannes' Church. The bus system contains a "nightline" that services local drinkeries.

www.traveldodo.com/webmaster/austria/feldkirch/

Hostel Feldkirch-Levis, Reichstr. 111, Feldkirch-Levis, Austria;
www.hihostels.com/, T:+43 552273181, *feldkirch@jungehotels.at*; $18 bed>,
Kitchen:Y, B'fast:$, WiFi:Y, Pvt. room:Y, Locker:Y, Desk hr:7a>11p;
Note: bar, parking, travel desk, luggage room, wheelchair, walk to train

INNSBRUCK has hosted the Winter Olympics more than once. Emperor Maximilian I used to live here. Landmarks include the Hofburg and the Franciscan, or Court, church. There are four major museums: the Ferdinandeum, the Tirolean Folk Art Museum; the Museum of the Imperial Rifles; and parts of the collections of the archduke Ferdinand II, in the Castle Ambras. Innsbruck is one of Europe's most popular resorts. It's the Alps.

www.innsbruck.info/

Y.H. Nikolaus Glockenhaus, Weiherburggasse 3, Innsbruck, Austria;
www.hostelnikolaus.at, T:0512286515, *innsbruck@hostelnikolaus.at*; $25 bed>,
Kitchen:N, B'fast:N, WiFi:$, Pvt. room:Y, Locker:N, Desk hr:9a>10p;
Note: close to center, good views

SALZBURG is best known for Mozart and *The Sound of Music*. There's more than that, though. The Old Town is a UNESCO World Heritage site. It includes the Residenzplatz, with a gallery of 16th-19th C. paintings, and the cathedral. Near Monchsberg (Monks' Hill) is the Benedictine Abbey of St. Peter and the Franciscan Church. The great fortress of Hohensalzburg crowns the hill. At times the tourists outnumber the locals.

www.salzburg.info/en

YoHo Intl. Youth Hostel, Paracelsusstraße 9, Salzburg, Austria;
www.yoho.at, T:0662879649, *office@yoho.at*; $24 bed>,
Kitchen:Y, B'fast:$, WiFi:Y, Pvt. room:Y, Locker:Y, Desk hr:24/7;
Note: bar, bike hire, laundry, luggage room, c.c. ok, afternoon kitchen

VIENNA is the capital and largest city of Austria, and home to fully one-fourth of Austria's eight-million- plus people. With Celtic roots and Roman rearing, it finally bore fruit as the city of the Habsburgs and de facto capital of the Holy Roman Empire, then Austria-Hungary. Perhaps more importantly, it was a world center of art and culture, particularly known for the music of Brahms, Mahler, and Strauss, but also for the analytic psychology of Freud, and the philosophy of Wittgenstein. The loss of empire and two world wars didn't change all that. Today its role as a center of culture extends to alternative culture, too. Notable landmarks include St. Stephan's Cathedral in the center, Church of the Augustinians, the Church of Maria am Gestade, and the Church of the Friars Minor, all dating from the 14th century. Even older is St. Ruprecht's. Secular buildings include the Imperial Palace, or Hofburg, with many museums. Vienna has the world's oldest zoo. For some reason most hostels here want payment in cash.

wien.gv.at/english/

Hostel Ruthensteiner, Robert-Hamerling-Gasse 24, Vienna, Austria;
www.*hostelruthensteiner.com,* T:018932796, *info@hostelruthensteiner.com*;
$25 bed>, Kitchen:Y, B'fast:$, WiFi:Y, Pvt. room:Y, Locker:Y, Desk hr:24/7;
Note: cash, bar, bike hire, luggage ok, travel desk, near train, walk>town

Palace Hostel Schlossherberge, Savoyenstrasse 2, Vienna, Austria,
www.hostel.at/en/, T:014810300, *shb@hostel.at*; $32bed>, Kitchen:N, B'fast:Y,
WiFi:Y, Pvt. room:Y, Locker:Y, Desk hr:lmtd;
Note: luggage room, laundry, parking, towel fee, mansion above city, far

Strawberry Y. H. Vienna, Mittelgasse 18, Vienna, Austria; *www.strawberryhostels.com/*, T:0159979660, *strawberryhostels@hotmail.com;* $29bed>, Kitchen:Y, B'fast:N, WiFi:Y, Pvt. room:Y, Locker:N, Desk hr:24/7; **Note:** no bunks, laundry, luggage room, travel desk, cash, central, hotel-like

Do Step Inn, Felberstrasse 20, Vienna, Austria; www.*dostepinn.com*, T:019823314, *office@dostepinn.com;* $24bed>,
Kitchen:Y, B'fast:N, WiFi:Y, Pvt. room:Y, Locker:N, Desk hr:lmtd;
Note: lounge, laundry, luggage room, close to train

Westend City Hostel, Fügergasse 3, Vienna, Austria; *www.westendhostel.at*, T:015976729, *info@westendhostel.at;* $27bed>, Kitchen:Y, B'fast:Y, WiFi:Y, Pvt. room:Y, Locker:Y, Desk hr:24/7; **Note:** cash only, laundry, lift to 10pm, luggage room, deposit p.p. for key

3) Belgium

Belgium exists as part of the historical uncertainty as to where the line is drawn between northern and southern Europe and what exactly that means. Part and parcel of that historical occurrence is the emergence of Belgium as continental Europe's first focus of the Industrial Revolution in the early 1800's. When Belgium seceded from the Netherlands in 1830, French speakers immediately formed the elite class, a situation which still causes problems to this day. French and Dutch (local dialects of the two) plus German, to a lesser extent, are the languages. Euro is currency. Phone code is +32.

www.visitbelgium.com/

ANTWERP has been a port of trade since time immemorial, a role it still fulfills today. As such, it has always been very much an international city. It inherited much of the trade that Bruges lost after its river silted up, and expanded on that with a banking industry very advanced for its time. Antwerp is also a center for Orthodox Jews, many involved in the diamond trade. Cultural amenities include the Royal Museum of Fine Arts, the National Maritime Museum, the Mayer van den Bergh Museum, the Museum of Contemporary Art, and the Middelheim Open-Air Museum of Sculpture. The performing arts are led by the Royal Flemish Opera House and by the Royal Dutch Theatre.

www.visitantwerpen.be

Alias Youth Hotel, Provinciestraat 256, Antwerpen, Belgium;
www.*wix.com/aliasyouthhostel/home*, T:032300522,
info@youthhotel.be; $25bed>, Kitchen:N, B'fast:Y, WiFi:Y, Pvt. room:Y,
Locker:Y, Desk hr:8a>5p;
Note: not central, full-time residents

BRUGES (Brugge) lies in a propitious site for trade, one it took full advantage of in the late Middle Ages. At the southern end of the Hanseatic routes and the northern end of the Genoese and Venetian ones, Bruges was the perfect conduit to funnel exotic Asian merchandise into the rapidly developing pre-Renaissance countries and economies of northern Europe. But Bruges couldn't maintain its advantage, or a silt-free channel, and by the late 1800's was being referred to as a "city of the dead." Thus was born its tourist industry, finding glory in a well-preserved past. Fortunately its medieval architecture survived the WWII nightmare relatively intact and today is a UNESCO world heritage site. It can be visited on a day-trip from Brussels. Medieval remains in the city include the old Market Hall and the Town Hall. Notable churches include the Cathedral of St. Salvator, the Church of Notre Dame, and the Church of Jerusalem. Museums include the Memling Museum in the 12th C. Hospital of St. John, the Groeninge Museum, and the 15th C. Gruuthuse mansion.

www.brugge.be

St. Christopher's Inn-Bauhaus, Langestraat 135, Brugge, Belgium;
www.bauhaus.be, T:050341093, *info@bauhaus.be*; $24bed>,
Kitchen:N, B'fast:Y, WiFi:Y, Pvt. room:Y, Locker:Y, Desk hr:24/7;
Note: bar, café, club, a/c, c.c. ok, bike hire, laundry, bunk curtain, loud bar

Snuffle Backpacker Hostel, Ezelstraat 47-49, Flanders, Bruges;
www.*snuffel.be*, T:050333133, *info@snuffel.be*; $21bed>,
Kitchen:Y, B'fast:Y, WiFi:Y, Pvt. room:N, Locker:N, Desk hr:lmtd;
Note: bar, left luggage, free tour, travel desk, c.c. ok, showers far/cold

Charlie Rockets, Hoogstraat 19, Brugge, Belgium;
www.charlierockets.com, T:050330660, *info@charlierockets.com*; $28bed>,

Kitchen:N, B'fast:$, WiFi:Y, Pvt. room:N, Locker:N, Desk hr:24/7;
Note: bar, restaurant, laundry c.c. ok, good location

BRUSSELS (Bruxelles) is Belgium's main city and largely a French-speaking enclave in Dutch-speaking Flanders. Maybe best known now as the capital of a now at-least-partially-united Europe, perhaps Brussels can accomplish for Europe what it has yet to accomplish for Belgium; perhaps. Cultural life includes the National Archive, the Albert I Royal Library, many museums and the Palace of Fine Arts. There is a red-light district that resembles Amsterdam without the canals. That's how you know it's a Dutch area, I guess. This is next to the largest Muslim area north of Tangier. Go figure.

www.brussels.com/

2GO4 Quality Hostel, Blvd Emile Jacqmain 99, Brussels;
www.2go4.be, T:022193019, *info@2go4.be*; $34bed>,
Kitchen:Y, B'fast:N, WiFi:Y, Pvt. room:Y, Locker:Y, Desk hr:8a>11p;
Note: dorm age 35, good location, check-in 4p, left luggage, real beds!

4) Denmark

The narrow conglomeration of continent and islands that connects Europe to Scandinavia is today the country of Denmark, a small area of land whose people changed the world around the beginning of the Common Era. For it was here that highly successful and populous Germanic tribes soon to become Franks, Lombards, Alemanni, Saxons, and Goths, etc. first pushed southward in an epic era of expansion and migration that first displaced the ubiquitous Celts, then many smaller groups, and finally even the powerful Romans themselves. Others of course went to England and displaced the Celts there. Denmark itself, though, remained most closely related to the northern countries and was part of the Viking era that rocked the world. Denmark was once in a union which included both Norway and Sweden, and still maintains oversight of Greenland and the Faroe Islands, which are otherwise self-governing today. Like Norway, Denmark has some North Sea oil that it exports. Politics tend to be environmental and progressive. The Danish *krone* is currency, Danish is the language, and the phone code is +45.

www.visitdenmark.us

COPENHAGEN is Denmark's capital and largest city. It has been a trading center since the Middle Ages, and was frequently attacked by the Hanseatic League. The straits that Denmark occupied between the Baltic and North Seas were prime passages to fuss over. They were later famously attacked by the British in 1807 and occupied by the Nazis in WWII. Things are calmer these days and Copenhagen has a rep as a modern and futuristic city, clean and green. In the center of the city is Tivoli Gardens, the second-oldest amusement park in the world, and featuring the oldest still-operating roller coaster and Ferris wheel in the world. The oldest amusement park is outside the city limits, Dyrehavsbakken in Klampenborg. Care for an apple, Mr. Disney?

Rådhuspladsen ("Town Hall Square") is the heart of the city, and other important buildings include Thott Palace, the Charlottenborg Palace, Christiansborg Palace, Bertel Thorvaldsen Museum, the Royal Arsenal Museum, the Royal Library, National Museum, the Church of Our Lady, the University of Copenhagen, the Petri Church, the 17th C. citadel, and the palace of Amalienborg. There is a major music festival at Roskilde. Via the recently-opened Oresund Bridge, Malmo in Sweden is now part of the metropolitan area of Copenhagen.

www.visitcopenhagen.com/

Danhostel Copenhagen Downtown, Vandkunsten 5, Copenhagen;
www.danhostel.dk/, T:28960699, *info@copenhagendowntown.com;*$29bed>,
Kitchen:Y, B'fast:$, WiFi:Y, Pvt. toom:Y, Locker:N, Desk hr:24/7;
Note: resto/bar, free laundry, forex, noisy bar

Generator Hostel Copenhagen, Adelgade 5, 1304 København, Denmark;
www.*generatorhostels.com,* T:78775400, *copenhagen@generatorhostels.com;*
$36bed>, Kitchen:Y, B'fast:N, WiFi:Y, Pvt. room:Y, Locker:Y, Desk hr:24/7;
Note: bar/café/club, lift, luggage ok, c.c. ok, big, new, neat, clean, central

Sleep in Heaven, Struensegade 7, København N, Denmark;
www.sleepinheaven.com/, T:35354648, *morefun@sleepinheaven.com;*
$23bed>, Kitchen:N, B'fast:$, WiFi:Y, Pvt. room:Y, Locker:Y, Desk hr:24/7;
Note: bar/café, luggage ok, tour, c.c.+4% surcharge, central

Danhostel Copenhagen City, H. C. Andersens Blvd. 50, København V;
www.danhostelcopenhagencity.dk, T:33118585; $26bed>,
Kitchen:Y, B'fast:$, WiFi:Y, Pvt. room:Y, Locker:Y, Desk hr:24/7;
Note: member discount, linen fee, confirm arrival 5p>, 17 floors, views

Hotel Jorgensen, Rømersgade 11, Copenhagen, Denmark;
www.hoteljoergensen.dk/, T:33138186, *HotelJoergensen@mail.dk*; $30bed>,
Kitchen:N, B'fast:$, WiFi:Y, Pvt. room:Y, Locker:N, Desk hr:24/7;
Note: c.c.+2.2%, bar, free tour, luggage ok, linen fee, central, near train

5) England

England makes up the bulk of the UK and is the economic engine and dominant player, if not necessarily the heart and soul, of the Kingdom. The history of the UK is first and foremost the history of England: the Anglo-Saxon invasion, the Danelaw, the Viking raids, the Norman Conquest, the Church of England, the Civil War, the Restoration, the Bill of Rights, the Empire, two World Wars, and perhaps the most incedible event of human history (still occurring to this day), the Industrial Revolution. This is probably England's greatest legacy to be left to the world. Pounds sterling (GBP) are currency, English is the language, and the calling code is +44.

www.visitbritain.com/

BATH is famous for its baths, of course, since it first came on the scene as a Roman spa town in 43 AD. It is a UNESCO World Heritage site, with Celtic baths, Roman baths, and then there's Thermae... The main landmark is the 16th C. abbey church of St. Peter and St. Paul. Then there are the 18th C. Pump Room, Queen Square, the Circus, the Guildhall, Lansdown Crescent, the Holburne of Menstrie Museum of Arts collection, and the Assembly Rooms, reopened in 1963 after destruction in WWII. Haile Selassie stayed here for four years.

www.visitbath.co.uk/

St. Christopher's Inn- Bath, 9 Green St, Bath, Somerset, England UK; st-christophers.co.uk/, T:02086007505, *feedback@st-christophers.co.uk*; $19bed>, Kitchen:N, B'fast:Y, WiFi:Y, Pvt. room:N, Locker:Y, Desk hr:lmtd; **Note:** resto/bar/café, tour desk, luggage room, laundry, central

YHA Bath, Bathwick Hill, Somerset, Bath, England UK; www.*yha.org.uk/hostel/bath*, T:08453719303, *bath@yha.org.uk*; $29bed>, Kitchen:Y, B'fast:$, WiFi:Y, Pvt. room:Y, Locker:Y, Desk hr:7a>11p; **Note:** 5 night max. stay, resto/bar, parking, c.c. ok, laundry

Bath Backpackers, 13 Pierrepont St, Bath, England UK; www.*hostels.co.uk*, T:+44(0)1225446787, *bath@hostels.co.uk*; $29bed>, Kitchen:Y, B'fast:N, WiFi:Y, Pvt. room:N, Locker:Y, Desk hr:lmtd; **Note:** tour desk, safe dep, c.c. ok, close to transport/center, party dungeon

BIRMINGHAM: If Manchester was the mill town of the Industrial Revolution, then Birmingham was the laboratory. The steam engine was invented here in 1776. That kept things running until petroleum and internal combustion took over, and without it the Industrial Revolution would've been impossible. Birmingham was a hotbed of small innovative workshops even before Manchester became the cheap-labor/mass-manufacture paradigm of industry. It was also the birthplace of heavy metal music. Now you know. Birmingham is England's second most populous city today. Landmarks include the classical Town Hall, the Renaissance-style Council House, the City of Birmingham Museum and Art Gallery, St. Philip's Cathedral, St. Paul's Church, St. Chad's Cathedral (Roman Catholic), Centenary Square, the International Convention Centre, and the Bullring shopping centre, likely the first thing you'll notice.

www.touruk.co.uk

B'ham Central Backpackers, 58 Coventry St. Birmingham, W. Midlands; *www.birminghamcentralbackpackers.com/*; T:01216430033; $20bed>, Kitchen:Y, B'fast:Y, WiFi:Y, Pvt. room:Y, Locker:Y, Desk hr:24/7; **Note:** near Nat. Express bus, bar, parking, c.c. ok, luggage ok, tour desk

Hatters Backpack Hostel, 92-95 Livery St, Jewellery Quarter, Birmingham; *www.hattersgroup.com/*, T:01212364031; $20bed>,
Kitchen:Y, B'fast:Y, WiFi:Y, Pvt. room:Y, Locker:N, Desk hr:24/7;
Note: wheelchairs ok, luggage ok, laundry, free tour, travel desk, c,c. ok

BRIGHTON is where you go to escape London, only a few hours away by train, and especially convenient if you've got business at Gatwick, home of the UK's second largest airport south of London. This is a party town; be forewarned. I suspect many of the guests are Brits from up-country. Double prices on weekends are not uncommon. It is also an art town, home of the annual Brighton Festival and its parallel Fringe Festival. Then there's the Soundwaves Festival, the Great Escape, Brighton Live, and the Brighton Pride festival for the LGBT community. It's irreverent; I warned you.

www.visitbrighton.com/

Kipps Hostel, 76 Grand Parade, Brighton, East Sussex, UK; *www.kipps-brighton.com/*, T:01273604182; $31bed>,
Kitchen:Y, B'fast:$, WiFi:Y, Pvt. room:Y, Locker:Y, Desk hr:9a-2a;
Note: bar, stairs, good location, terrace, coffee and tea, terrace, parties

Sobo House, 10-11 Seafield Rd., Brighton, E. Sussex, UK; *www.roomsinbrighton.co.uk/*, T:01273323097,
info@roomsinbrighton.co.uk; $19bed>,
Kitchen:Y, B'fast:$, WiFi:Y, Pvt. room:Y, Locker:Y, Desk hr:24/7;
Note: laundry, TV, dog, double price on weekends

St. Cristopher's, 10-12 Grand Junction Rd, Brighton, UK;
www.*st-christophers.co.uk/*, T:+44(0)1273202035; $33bed>,
Kitchen:N, B'fast:Y, WiFi:Y, Pvt. room:Y, Locker:Y, Desk hr:lmtd;
Note: bar/club, late noise, close to pier, nice views

Grapevine North Laine, 29/30 North Rd, Brighton, UK;
www.grapevinewebsite.co.uk, T:01273777717, *enquiry@grapevinewebsite.co.uk;*
$24bed>, Kitchen:Y, B'fast:N, WiFi:Y, Pvt. room:N, Locker:N, Desk hr:9a>6p;
Note: nice location, near station

Journeys, 33 Richmond Pl, Brighton and Hove, E. Sussex, UK; *www.visitjourneys.com/*, T:01273695866; $24bed>, Kitchen:Y, B'fast:Y, WiFi:Y, Pvt. room:N, Locker:Y, Desk hr:24/7; **Note:** laundry, TV, curtained 3-deck bunks w/ socket & light

BRISTOL is situated in the south of England, so a bit warmer than most towns. It has long been a major English port, second only to Liverpool. In the medieval era it was one of England's three most important cities until the rise of the Midlands during the Industrial Revolution. Landmarks include the cathedral church; St. Mark's; the Dominican priory of William Penn; the New Room in Broadmead; Broadmead Baptist Chapel; and the Theatre Royal, built in 1766.

www.visitbristol.co.uk/

YHA, 14 Narrow Quay, Bristol, Avon, United Kingdom; www.*yha.org.uk/*, T:08453719726, *bristol@yha.org.uk*; $30bed>, Kitchen:Y, B'fast:$, WiFi:$, Pvt. room:Y, Locker:Y, Desk hr:24/7; **Note:** 5 night max. stay, bar, c.c. ok, central, towel fee, member discount

Full Moon and Attic Bar, 1 North St., Stokes Croft, Bristol, UK; *www.fmbristol.co.uk/*, T:01179245007, *info@fullmoonbristol.co.uk*; $28bed>, Kitchen:Y, B'fast:N, WiFi:Y, Pvt. room:N, Locker:N, Desk hr:>11p; **Note:** resto/bar, wheelchair ok, parking, c.c. ok, close to bus/center

007 Travellers Hostel, 150 West St, Bedminster, *Bristol* UK; *www.007hostel.net/*, T:+4401179662936, *info@007hostel.net*; $20bed>, Kitchen:Y, B'fast:N, WiFi:Y, Pvt. room:N, Locker:Y, Desk hr:24/7; **Note:** weekly rates, luggage room, c.c. ok, TV, coffee & tea, not central

LIVERPOOL can only mean one thing, of course, to anyone who lived during this side of the previous century, but there's a little more to it than just the Beatles. At one point 40% of the world's trade passed through the port of Liverpool. That brought in people from all over the world, including UK's oldest Chinese and black African communities, and scads of Irish. Much of this trade was in the fruit of Manchester's looms, but much was also in slaves. With the UK's decline in manufacturing prowess, Liverpool saw a sharp decline in prosperity and much unemployment. It is a long-term problem that defies easy solution. The Tate Liverpool, Merseyside County Museum and Library, the Walker Art Gallery, the Picton Library, and the University of Liverpool are among the cultural institutions. This is a point of embarkation for ferries to Ireland and the Isle of Man.

www.visitliverpool.com/

Hatters Liverpool, 56/60 Mount Pleasant, Liverpool, UK;
www.*hattersgroup.com/*, T:+44(0)1517095570; $26bed>,
Kitchen:Y, B'fast:Y, WiFi:$, Pvt. room:Y, Locker:N, Desk hr:24/7;
Note: laundry, c.c. ok, towel fee, partying teenagers, 2 night min. stay

Embassie Liverpool Backpackers, 1 Falkner Sq, Liverpool UK;
www.embassie.com/, T:01517071089, reservations@embassie.com; $29bed>,
Kitchen:Y, B'fast:Y, WiFi:Y, Pvt. room:N, Locker:$, Desk hr:24/7;
Note: min. stay 2N, free Beatles tour, some noise

YHA Liverpool, 25 Tabley St, off Wapping, Merseyside, Liverpool UK;
www.*yha.org.uk/*, T:08453719527, *liverpool@yha.org.uk*; $26bed>,
Kitchen:Y, B'fast:$, WiFi:$, Pvt. room:Y, Locker:N, Desk hr:24/7;
Note: c.c. ok, laundry, surcharge for non-members

International Inn, 4 South Hunter St., Liverpool, Merseyside, UK;
www.*internationalinn.co.uk/* T:01517098135, *info@internationalinn.co.uk*;
$28bed>, Kitchen:Y, B'fast:Y, WiFi:Y, Pvt. room:N, Locker:N, Desk hr:24/7;
Note: near train

Everton Hostel, 53 Everton Rd, Liverpool, Merseyside, UK;
www.*everton.hostel.com/*, T:+44(0)7916495468; $23bed>,
Kitchen:Y, B'fast:Y, WiFi:Y, Pvt. room:N, Locker:Y, Desk hr:3p>10p;
Note: call 1 hr before arrive, cash only, laundry, lots of extras

LONDON is the capital and largest city of England, and one of the great cities in the history of the world. What can you say about London that hasn't already been said? It's huge, sprawling, magnificent, and once controlled about half the world. The Romans founded it in 43 AD as Londinium on the River Thames, from which it grew to become the largest city in the world for almost a hundred years. To this day it's the best place from which to access the rest of the world, somewhat equidistant to all the rest, economically if not geographically. You can easily spend a few days sight-seeing here. Major tourist attractions include the famous Houses of Parliament, Buckingham Palace, Big Ben and Westminster Abbey. That should keep you busy. If not, then check out the British Museum, the National Gallery, Madame Tussaud's wax museum, and the three major South Kensington museums (Victoria and Albert, Natural History, and Science).

Then there are the Tower Bridge, the Tower of London, the London Eye, St. Paul's Cathedral, Borough Market, Shakespeare's Globe Theatre and the Tate Modern Art Gallery. Tired yet? Trafalgar Square is more or less in the center of the cookie jar. Wear good shoes. Hostels are numerous and good, but be aware that many non-travelers use London hostels as a base for party weekends. There seems to be a lot of consolidation in the London market, too, chains now dominating the hostel scene, with ensuing price rises.

www.london.gov.uk

YHA London Central, 104-108 Bolsover St, Marylebone, London, UK; www.yha.org.uk, T:08453719154, *londoncentral@yha.org.uk*; $44bed>, Kitchen:Y, B'fast:$, WiFi:$, Pvt. room:Y, Locker:Y, Desk hr:24/7;
Note: laundry, bar, plenty of power outlets

The Green Man, 308 Edgeware Rd, London, England, UK; www.*bestplaceinns.com/*, T:02077237980, *greenman@bestplaceinns.com*; $39bed>, Kitchen:N, B'fast:Y, WiFi:Y, Pvt. room:N, Locker:Y, Desk hr:24/7;
Note: good 24 hr. pub, laundry, age 18>, free walking tour, towel fee

YHA London St. Pancras, 79-81 Euston Road, London, UK; www.*yha.org.uk/*, T:08453719344, *stpancras@yha.org.uk*; $45bed>, Kitchen:N, B'fast:$, WiFi:$, Pvt. room:Y, Locker:Y, Desk hr:24/7;
Note: bar, surcharge for non-HI/YHA members, convenient for Eurostar

White Ferry House-Victoria, 1A Sutherland St, Victoria, London, UK; www.*bestplaceinns.com/*, T:02072336133, *whiteferry@bestplaceinns.com*; $35bed>, Kitchen:Y, B'fast:Y, WiFi:Y, Pvt. room:N, Locker:Y, Desk hr:24/7;
Note: pub downstairs, close to Victoria Coach Station, 3-decker bunks

Palmer's Lodge Swiss Cottage, 40 College Crescent, London, UK; www.*palmerslodges.com/*, T:02072244405; $26bed>, Kitchen:N, B'fast:Y, WiFi:Y, Pvt. room:N, Locker:Y, Desk hr:24/7; **Note:** laundry, bar & restaurant available, towel fee

The Great Eastern, 1 Glenaffric Avenue, London, England UK; www.*bestplaceinns.com/*, T:02075316514, *greateastern@bestplaceinns.com*; $33bed>, Kitchen:Y, B'fast:Y, WiFi:Y, Pvt. room:N, Locker:N, Desk hr:24/7; **Note:** min. age 18>, bar/café, far out by Greenwich, quiet neighborhood

Clink 261, 265 Gray's Inn Rd, London, UK; www.*ashleehouse.co.uk/*, T:02078339400, *info@ashleehouse.co.uk*; $37bed>, Kitchen:Y, B'fast:Y, WiFi:$, Pvt. room:N, Locker:N, Desk hr:24/7; **Note:** "mainly 18-35 y.o. backpackers" wanted

Palmer's Lodge Hillspring, 233 Willesden Lane, London UK; www.*palmerslodges.com/*, T:02070992435; $26bed>, Kitchen:N, B'fast:Y, WiFi:Y, Pvt. room:Y, Locker:N, Desk hr:24/7; **Note:** bar & restaurant, laundry, a bit distant

Walrus Waterloo, 172 Westminster Bridge Rd., London, UK; www.*walrussocial.com/*, T:02079284368; $35bed>, Kitchen:N, B'fast:Y, WiFi:Y, Pvt. room:N, Locker:Y, Desk hr:7a>11p; **Note:** downstairs pub, good location, some noise

Generator Hostel, Compton Pl. off 37 Tavistock Pl., London UK; www.*generatorhostels.com/*, T:02073887655, *london@generatorhostels.com*; $48bed>, Kitchen:N, B'fast:$, WiFi:$, Pvt. room:Y, Locker:Y, Desk hr:24/7; **Note:** min. stay 3 nights, bar, "party every night," laundry, towel fee

Astor Quest Hostel, 45 Queensborough Terrace, Bayswater, London, UK; www.*astorhostels.co.uk/*, T:+44(0)2072297782; $23bed>, Kitchen:Y, B'fast:Y, WiFi:$, Pvt. room:N, Locker:Y, Desk hr:24/7; **Note:** age 18-35 only, few sockets, towel fee

Monkeys in the Trees, 49 Becklow Rd, Shepherds Bush, London, UK; www.*monkeysinthetrees.co.uk/*, T:02087499197,

info@monkeysinthetrees.co.uk; $29bed>, Kitchen:Y, B'fast:Y, WiFi:Y, Pvt. room:N, Locker:, Desk hr:>11p;
Note: min. stay 2 nights, towel fee, bar downstairs, nice 'hood but a bit far

YHA London St. Paul's, 36 Carter Lane, London, England, UK; www.*yha.org.uk*, T:02072364965, *stpauls@yha.org.uk*; $:41bed>, Kitchen:N, B'fast:$, WiFi:$, Pvt. room:Y, Locker:N, Desk hr:24/7;
Note: bar & restaurant, c.c. ok, surcharges for non-members

St. Christopher's, 28 Hammersmith Broadway, London, UK; www.*st-christophers.co.uk*, T:02087485285, *bookings@st-christophers.co.uk*; $17bed>, Kitchen:N, B'fast:Y, WiFi:Y, Pvt. room:N, Locker:N, Desk hr:24/7; Note: party bar downstairs, no computers, min. stay 2 nights

Equity Point, 100-102 Westbourne Terrace, London, England UK; www.*equity-point.com/*, T:02070878001; $:41bed>, Kitchen:Y, B'fast:Y, WiFi:$, Pvt. room:Y, Locker:Y, Desk hr:24/7;
Note: bar & café, towel fee, c.c. ok

Travel Joy Hostel, The King William IV, 111 Grosvenor Rd, London; www.*traveljoyhostels.com/*, T:02078349689, *info@traveljoyhostels.com*; $44bed>, Kitchen:N, B'fast:Y, WiFi:Y, Pvt. room:Y, Locker:Y, Desk hr:lmtd;
Note: Thai resto/bar, café, free tour, travel desk, luggage ok, parking

Smart Russell Square, 71 Guilford St, London, England, UK; www.*smartbackpackers.com*, T:02078338818, *srs.bookings@smartbackpackers.com*; $18bed>, Kitchen:Y, B'fast:Y, WiFi:Y, Pvt. room:Y, Locker:Y, Desk hr:24/7;
Note: c.c. chg +5%, tour desk, laundry, parking, forex, ages 16-60

The Antigallican Hotel, 428 Woolwich Rd, Charlton, London UK; www.*antigallicanhotel.com/*, T:02088530143, *info@antigallicanhotel.com*; $23bed>, Kitchen:Y, B'fast:N, WiFi:Y, Pvt. room:Y, Locker:Y, Desk hr:24/7;
Note: close to O2 dome, bar, luggage room, laundry, parking, c.c. ok

Globe Trott Inns, 1 Barking Rd, London, England UK; www.*globetrott-inns.com/*, T:07723580911, *globetrottinns@gmail.com*; $18bed>, Kitchen:N, B'fast:Y, Wi-Fi:Y, Pvt. room:N, Locker:Y, Desk hr:>10p;
Note: bar, ATM, luggage ok, laundry, tour desk, not central, few sockets

Dover Castle Hostel, 6A Great Dover St, London, England UK; www.*dovercastlehostel.com/*, T:02074037773, info@dovercastlehostel.com; $18bed>, Kitchen:Y, B'fast:Y, WiFi:Y, Pvt. room:N, Locker:$, Desk hr:24/7;
Note: bar, free tour, travel desk, luggage room, laundry, TV, forex, c.c. ok

New Cross Inn, 323 New Cross Road, Greater London UK; www.*newcrossinn.co.uk/*, T:02083554976; $23bed>, Kitchen:Y, B'fast:Y, WiFi:Y, Pvt. room:Y, Locker:$, Desk hr:24/7;
Note: bar, parking, tour desk, luggage ok, laundry, a/c, c.c. ok, age 18-40

The Steam Engine, 41-42 Cosser St, London, England UK; www.*thesteamenginehostel.co.uk*, T:02079280720, *steamengine@bestplaceinns.com*; $23bed>, Kitchen:N, B'fast:Y, WiFi:Y, Pvt. room:N, Locker:Y, Desk hr:24/7;
Note: towel fee, free tour, 24 hr bar, c.c. ok, 3-deck bunks

Journeys Kings Cross Hostel, 54-58 Caledonian Rd, London UK; www.*visitjourneys.com*, T:0207833393, kingscross@visitjourneys.com; $31bed>, Kitchen:Y, B'fast:Y, WiFi:Y, Pvt. room:Y, Locker:Y, Desk hr:24/7;
Note: free tour, travel desk, luggage room, TV

Arsenal Tavern Hostel, 175 Blackstock Rd, London UK; www.*arsenaltavern.com* T:02073596902, *arsenaltavern@gmail.com*; $18bed>, Kitchen:N, B'fast:Y, WiFi:Y, Pvt. room:N, Locker:Y, Desk hr:24/7;
Note: cash only, resto/bar, lounge, luggage room

Strand Continental, 143 Strand, London, England UK; www.*strand-continental.co.uk*, T:02078364880, *strandcontinentalhotel@gmail.com*; $36bed>,

Kitchen:N, B'fast:Y, WiFi:Y, Pvt. room:Y, Locker:N, Desk hr:24/7;
Note: 6 Fl no lift, resto/bar, safe deposit, luggage ok, c.c. ok, prime loc.

Surprise Backpackers, 110 Vauxhall Bridge Rd, London UK;
www.*surprisebackpackers.com/*, T:02078288620; $26bed>
Kitchen:Y, B'fast:Y, WiFi:Y, Pvt. room:N,
Locker:Y, Desk hr:8a>11p;
Note: bar, lounge, TV, luggage ok, c.c. ok, close to Victoria, few sockets

The Court Hostel, 194-196 Earl's Court Rd, London UK;
www.*nightsinn.co.uk*, T:02073730027,
TheCourtHostel@hotmail.com; $29bed>, Kitchen:Y, B'fast:Y,
WiFi:Y, Pvt. room:Y, Locker:Y, Desk hr:24/7;
Note: cash only, free tour, travel desk, luggage ok, safe deposit, coffee/tea

Royal Bayswater, 121 Bayswater Rd, London UK;
www.*royalbayswater.com*, T:+44(0)2072298888,
bookings@royalbayswater.com; $20bed>, Kitchen:Y, B'fast:Y,
WiFi:N, Pvt. room:N, Locker:$, Desk hr:24/7;
Note: restaurant, tour desk, forex, safe deposit, towel & left luggage fee

Piccadilly Backpackers Hostel, 12 Sherwood St, Greater London UK;
www.*piccadillyhotel.net/*, T:02074349009,
bookings@piccadillyhotel.net; $22bed>, Kitchen:N, B'fast:$,
WiFi:$, Pvt. room:Y, Locker:Y, Desk hr:24/7;
Note: c.c. ok, good location

Barkston Youth Hostel, 1 Barkston Gardens, Earl's Court, London UK;
www.*barkstonyouthhostel.com*; T:02073734322; $31bed>,
Kitchen:Y, B'fast:$, WiFi:$, Pvt. room:Y, Locker:N, Desk hr:24/7;
Note: luggage room, laundry, c.c. ok, good location

Brazen Backpackers, 69 Lisson St, London UK;
www.*brazenbackpackers.com*, T:02077235077; $26bed>,
Kitchen:Y, B'fast:Y, WiFi:Y, Pvt. room:N, Locker:Y, Desk hr:lmtd;
Note: resto/bar, luggage room, laundry, c.c. ok

MANCHESTER is the world's first industrialized city, maybe a dubious claim in a port-industrial Britain, but significant in world history. This industry was based on textile production and related support industries, including the cotton trade from ya'll-know-where. That also means chemicals, dyes, canals, railways, and machines, lots of them. It was also the scene of bread and labor riots. Marx met Engels here. The rest is history. The Royal Exchange now houses a freestanding theatre-in-the-round. The old Central Station has been converted into an exhibition centre. A complex of buildings at Castlefield has been developed as a regional museum of science and industry. Other museums include the Whitworth Art Gallery, the Manchester City Art Gallery, the Manchester Museum, and the Museum of Science and Industry. Since a 1996 IRA bombing that injured two hundred people, Manchester has renovated and reinvented itself. Now its economy is largely service-oriented. It has also much nightlife.

www.manchester.com

Hatters on Newton, 50 Newton St., Greater Manchester UK;
www.*hattersgroup.com*, T:+44(0)1612369500; $27bed>,
Kitchen:Y, B'fast:Y, WiFi:Y, Pvt. room:N, Locker:Y, Desk hr:24/7;
Note: close to bus & train, coffee & tea, c.c. necessary, no lift

Hatters at Hilton Chambers, 15 Hilton St, Manchester, England UK;
www.h*attersgroup.com*, T:+44(0)1612364414; $31bed>,
Kitchen:Y, B'fast:Y, WiFi:Y, Pvt. room:N, Locker:N, Desk hr:24/7;
Note: luggage room, safe deposit, c.c. necessary, non-party

YHA Manchester, Potato Wharf, Castlefield, Manchester UK;
www.*yha.org.uk/*, T:08453719647; $32bed>,
Kitchen:Y, B'fast:$, WiFi:$, Pvt. room:Y, Locker:Y, Desk hr:24/7;
Note: resto/bar, tour desk, parking, towel/luggage room/membership fee

NOTTINGHAM during the Industrial Revolution was known for its lace and its slums, but most visitors are attracted by the legend of Robinhood and Sherwood Forest, of which a remnant still remains. It used to be ruled by a Saxon chief named Snot. The old Saxon town is marked by a castle on Standard

Hill, which now houses a museum. The old market square dominates the center. There have been race riots.

www.nottinghamtouristguide.co.uk/

Igloo Backpackers Hostel, 110 Mansfield Rd, Nottingham UK;
www.*igloohostel.co.uk/*, T:01159475250, *info@igloohostel.co.uk*; $26bed>,
Kitchen:Y, B'fast:N, WiFi:Y, Pvt. room:Y, Locker:Y, Desk hr:>1a;
Note: luggage room, laundry, tour desk, c.c. ok, long stay ok, central

Midtown Hostel, 5A Thurland St, Nottingham, England UK;
www.*midtownhostel.co.uk*, T:01159410150, *book@midtownhostel.co.uk*; $24bed>
Kitchen:Y, B'fast:N, Wi-Fi:Y, Pvt. room:Y, Locker:N, Desk hr:24/7;
Note: laundry, c.c. ok, tea & coffee, central

OXFORD began its history in Saxon times as a ford for oxen (yep), long before it became famous as a university town in the 12th century. Radical clerics were burnt at the stake here in 1555. At only 50mi/80km from London, it's an easy day trip either way. Matthew Arnold called it "the city of dreaming spires." I like that. Most of them belong to the university, and were built in the 15th, 16th, and 17th centuries. Oxford is also famous for its breweries. It has one of the highest rates of ethnic diversity in England.

www.visitoxfordandoxfordshire.com/

Central Backpackers Oxford, 13 Park End St, Oxford UK;
www.*centralbackpackers.co.uk/*, T:01865242288,
oxford@centralbackpackers.co.uk; $32bed>, Kitchen:Y, B'fast:Y,
WiFi:Y, Pvt. room:N, Locker:Y, Desk hr:8a>11p;
Note: luggage room, laundry, tour desk, c.c. ok, central

Oxford Backpackers, 9A Hythe Bridge Street, Oxford, UK;
www.*hostels.co.uk/oxford.php*, T:01865721761, *oxford@hostels.co.uk*; $29>,
Kitchen:Y, B'fast:Y, WiFi:Y, Pvt. room:N, Locker:Y, Desk hr:8a>11p;
Note: bar, printer, fax, many power sockets, tea/coffee, close to bus/train

6) Faroe Islands

The Faroe Islands are a self-governing country of 50,000 people of ethnic Norse and Gaelic descent functioning under the umbrella of Denmark (it rains a lot). It lies about halfway between Norway and Iceland, and though it shares many adjectives with Iceland, it also has its own culture and language, based on Old Norse. Fishing is the traditional occupation, but that is changing with new information technologies. There are festivals in the summer. The capital is Torshavn. The languages are Danish and Faroese. The currencies are Danish *krone* and Faroese *krona*. The telephone country code is +298.

www.visitfaroeislands.com/

ORAVIK is a village on the island of Suduroy. It's not the capital or largest city of the Faroes, but in a country of 50,000, that doesn't mean much. If you visit Oravik, the population will increase approximately 2.5%. The ferry will take you there.

Hotel Oravik, 827 Øravik, Faroe Islands;
www.*oravik.com* T:+298371302; $20bed>, Kitchen:Y, B'fast:$,
WiFi:N, Pvt. room:N, Locker:N, Desk hr:lmtd;
Note: high linen/towel fee, tour desk, c.c. ok

7) Finland

Finns are related to the original inhabitants of Scandinavia and other tribal groups that inhabited the vast northern lands between the Urals and the Atlantic, and if linguistics imply races, maybe all the way to the Altai four-corners region where China meets Russia meets Kazakhstan meets Mongolia. After being colonized for centuries by Sweden until Russia took a turn in the 1800's, Finland finally achieved total independence last century, with a distinct policy of not bugging the Russians. Now they are a full-fledged member of modern Europe and modern Scandinavia, and the only one of them using the Euro as currency. The first work written in Finnish was the New Testament in the 16th century. *Kalevala* is the national folk epic. There is a lively music and arts scene. The phone code is +358 and Finnish, Swedish, and Sami are the languages.

www.visitfinland.com

HELSINKI is the capital and largest city in Finland, and home to approximately twenty percent of all Finns. Though founded in 1550, it didn't grow much until the 19th century. Today it is less expensive than the other Scandinavian capitals, so not a bad place to hang for a while. There are ferry services to Stockholm, St. Petersburg and Tallinn only some 50mi/80km across the water in Estonia. The city is small enough to walk around easily and the architecture is lovely. Much of it is clustered around Senate Square, such as the state council building and the Lutheran cathedral. Uspenski Orthodox Cathedral is a vestige of previous Russian rule. In the Hollywood tradition of "day for night," Helsinki has been used frequently in cold-war movies as the cinematic equivalent of Communist USSR, art imitating life. This is the place to try a reindeer burger. Enjoy.

www.visithelsinki.fi/en

Eurohostel, Linnankatu 9, Helsinki, Finland; www.*eurohostel.eu/*, T:096220470, *eurohostel@eurohostel.fi*; $35bed>,
Kitchen:Y, B'fast:$, WiFi:$, Pvt. room:Y, Locker:Y, Desk hr:24/7;
Note: restaurant, luggage room, laundry, c.c. ok, free sauna, central

Stadion, Pohjoinen Stadiontie, Helsinki, Finland;
www.stadionhostel.fi/, T:094778480, *info@stadionhostel.fi*; $29bed>,
Kitchen:Y, B'fast:$, WiFi:Y, Pvt. room:Y, Locker:Y, Desk hr:24/7;
Note: HI member discount, laundry, luggage ok, c.c. ok, non-party, far

8) France

The area now occupied by France was a Celtic region during the days of the Roman Empire, when a Gallic-Roman Latin-speaking culture was forged. After the fall of Rome and the invasion by Germanic tribes, the victorious Franks gradually absorbed that culture as their own and successfully parlayed that stable population base into Europe's first great post-Roman empire, the Carolingian one of Charlemagne which ruled the area until almost 1000 in a proto-Holy Roman Empire. Around that time the Holy Roman Empire shifted eastward into German lands, while a united French kingdom gradually began to emerge in the decentralized feudal countryside. Viking invasions were a major problem and the Crusades were a major diversion at this time. Monarchs ruled until the end of the 18th century, when the French revolution set a course of events into motion the effects of which are still being felt to this day.

France became a major colonial power, and arguably the only one to successfully integrate those colonies as overseas departments into a modern state. France is one of the greenest of modern developed countries and one of the more equitable and socially balanced. At the same time it maintains a large military defense and space industry. Spanning both north and south Europe, in many ways it IS the symbol of Europe, and a European Union without France at the center of it is unthinkable. It is the most visited country in the world, for its mountains, its beaches, and Paris. Travel here is mostly by train, some of them very fast (TGV). Buses are mostly for very local and Eurolines international service. Hostels are relatively few, unfortunately, boo hoo. Euro is the currency. Telephone country code is +33. French is the language.

www.us.franceguide.com/

CHAMONIX: Chamonix was the site of the first winter Olympics in 1924. Situated at only a little over 1000 meters (3400 feet), the surrounding peaks rise to almost 5000 meters, including Mont Blanc at 4807 (15,771 feet). The highest cable-car system in the world is located here. In summer it is a mecca for mountain bikers.

www.chamonix.com

Hostel Le Chamoniard Volant, 45 Route de la Frasse, Chamonix;
www.*chamoniard.com,* T:+33450531409, *mail@chamoniard.com;* $20bed>,
Kitchen:Y, B'fast:$, WiFi:Y, Pvt. room:N, Locker:Y, Desk hr:10a>10p;
Note: close to train/center, restaurant/café, parking, c.c. ok, 7-day cancel

MARSEILLES is France's second-largest city and largest on the Mediterranean coast. It is also France's oldest city, founded by the Greeks as Massalia before it became Roman as Massilia. After the fall of Rome, the Visigoths took over briefly before the Franks and Charlemagne came in, then the counts of Provence. It was reincorporated into France in the 15th century and served as naval base for the Franco-Ottoman alliance. As a major port it suffered badly during the various plagues and was always at odds with authority. It strongly supported the French revolution and more recent socialist and communist political movements. They say Mary Magdalene and Lazarus preached the Gospel here.

Fort St. Jean overlooks the harbor and was a 13th C. outpost of the Knights Hospitaller. Fort Saint-Nicholas occupies the other side. The Place de la Major holds the city's cathedral and dates from the 11th century. So does the square-towered basilica of Saint-Victor. Notre-Dame-de-la-Garde stands high on the hill over the south side of the port. Marseilles couldn't be more different from Paris. If Paris is up and stuffy, then Marseilles is down and dirty. This is where Europe meets the Middle East, and where Europe meets Africa. Maybe 25% of the population is Muslim. Maybe 10% is Jewish. Algerian *'rai'* musicians do here what they can't do back home; so do the Guineans. Cheap rooms are a tradition, with or without baths. You can try the local *hammam* for that. But hostels are better.

www.marseille-tourisme.com/en

Hotel Vertigo Vieux Port, 38 rue Fort Notre Dame, Marseille, France; www.*hotelvertigo.fr*, T:0491544295, *contact-vieuxport@hotelvertigo.fr*; $34bed>, Kitchen:Y, B'fast:Y, WiFi:Y, Pvt. room:N, Locker:Y, Desk hr:24/7;
Note: luggage room, tour desk, a/c, c.c. ok, good location

Hello Marseille, 12 rue de Breteuil, Marseille, France; www.*hellomarseille.com/*, T:0954807505, *hellomarseille@gmail.com*; $26bed>, Kitchen:Y, B'fast:Y, WiFi:Y, Pvt. room:N, Locker:Y, Desk hr:24/7;
Note: luggage room, laundry, c.c. ok, stairs, central

London Connection Hostel, 45 Rue Flegier, Marseille, France; www.*london-connect.com/*, T:+33699014149, *londonconnect@yahoo.fr*; $30bed>, Kitchen:Y, B'fast:Y, WiFi:Y, Pvt. room:N, Locker:N, Desk hr:>12a;
Note: 30 night max. stay, coffee & tea, tour desk, laundry, 30-day cancel

Vertigo Hostel, 42 Rue des Petites Maries, Marseille, Côte d'Azur, France; www.*hotelvertigo.fr*, T:+33(0)491910711, *contact@hotelvertigo.fr*; $34bed>, Kitchen:N, B'fast:$, WiFi:Y, Pvt. room:N, Locker:N, Desk hr:24/7;
Note: bar, tour desk, luggage room, laundry, c.c. ok, no lift, close to train

Hostel Sylvabelle Marseille, 63 Rue Sylvabelle, Marseille, France; www.*hotel-sylvabelle-marseille.com*; T:0491377583; $33bed>, Kitchen:N, B'fast:N, WiFi:Y, Pvt. room:Y, Locker:N, Desk hr:24/7;
Note: c.c. ok, no lift, curfew, some confusion between hotel & hostel

NICE is the heart of the French Riviera. The beach is the big deal here, but Monaco is nearby, and Italy not much farther. In fact much of Nice's history lies with Italy, not France. Founded by Greeks before the Common Era it was in league with Genoa and/or Pisa after the Fall of Rome and in constant struggle against the Arabs and later Barbary pirates. It was finally ceded to France in 1860, though Italy reoccupied it in WWII. Things are calmer now, and tourism is king. Blessed with coastal beaches, nearby mountains and mild winters, Nice attracts visitors and immigrants from all over the world. There is an old town with narrow winding streets and a harbor with regular boat service to the island of Corsica. The Musee' des Beaux Arts and the Musee' Massena specialize in paintings. Northeast of the center is the ancient Episcopal town of Cimiez, with Roman ruins. Hostel quality is uneven in the French style, but quite passable.

en.nicetourisme.com/

Villa Saint Exupery Gardens, 22 Avenue Gravier, Nice, France;
www.*villahostels.com/index-en,* T:0493844283,
gardens@villahostels.com; $24bed>, Kitchen:Y, B'fast:Y,
WiFi:Y, Pvt. room:Y,
Locker:Y, Desk hr:24/7;
Note: a/c, c.c. ok, forex, resto/bar, free tour, parking, big old house in hills

Hostel Paradis, Rue Paradis, Nice, France;
www.paradishotel.com/, T:0493877123, *hotelparadisnice@gmail.com*; $37bed>,
Kitchen:N, B'fast:$, WiFi:Y, Pvt. room:Y, Locker:N, Desk hr:>8p;
Note: c.c. ok, no bunks, on beach, in-room fridge, more like hotel

Hostel Meyerbeer Beach, 15 Rue Meyerbeer, Nice, France;
www.*hotel-meyerbeer-beach-nice.cote.azur.fr/*, T:0493889565; $40bed>,
Kitchen:Y, B'fast:Y, WiFi:Y, Pvt. room:Y, Locker:N, Desk hr:>12m;
Note: a/c, c.c. ok, travel desk, near beach, cheap wine for sale

Altea Hostel, 3 Boulevard Raimbaldi, Nice, France;
www.*hostel-nice.com/*, T:0493851522, *Info@Hostel-Nice.com*; $48bed>,
Kitchen:N, B'fast:N, WiFi:Y, Pvt. room:Y, Locker:N, Desk hr:8a>11p;
Note: fridge & microwave, near train, walk to beach

Villa St. Exupery Beach, 6 Rue Sacha Guitry, Nice, France;
www.*villahostels.com/index-en*, T:0493161345,
beach@villahostels.com; $39bed>, Kitchen:Y, B'fast:Y,

WiFi:Y, Pvt. room:Y, Locker:N, Desk hr:24/7;
Note: bar, forex, c.c. ok, a/c, free tour, coffee & tea, heart of the city

PARIS is the largest city, capital, and heart of the French republic, of course, and got its start as capital of the Frankish Merovingian dynasty in the year 508. After losing that role, it returned as capital of the first Capetian kindon in 987, a role it held for most of the next thousand years with France. After much political uncertainty with the French Revolution and Napoleon, Paris finally entered the Industrial Revolution with the 1852 Second Republic, and in a way that differed greatly from the misery of it elsewhere. Paris was rapidly gaining a reputation as a city with a difference, a view only heightened by the Commune established after defeat in the Franco-Prussian War. If that was ultimately a disaster, the Expositions of 1889 and 1900 were anything but. The Eiffel Tower was a raging success, the Paris Metro was built, electric lights were installed, and the "city of lights" with a reputation as the most romantic city in the world was born. I don't know about all that, but it certainly has plenty to offer a tourist.

Much of Paris has been declared a UN World Heritage site, to mention but a few of the main sights: the Eiffel Tower, the Louvre Museum, Notre Dame Cathedral, the Arc d' Triomphe, the Pont Neuf, the Place Dauphine, the Palace of Justice, the Grand Chambre, the Sainte-Chapelle, the Tuileries Garden, the Musee Orsay, the Champs-Elysees, the Hotel des Invalides, the Quartier Latin, the Pantheon, the Hotel de Ville, the Paris Opera House, les Places des Concorde et Pyramides, dozens of museums and much more. Better develop an espresso habit in order to see it all. They're cheap, as long as you don't sit down. Unfortunately, it doesn't have the number of hostels that many of the other largest cities in Europe have, and what they have are not as high quality. Many of them are clustered in Montmartre.

www.paris.fr/

Le Village Hostel, 20 Rue d'Orsel, Paris, Île-de-France, France;
www.villagehostel.fr/, T:+33142642202, bonjour@villagehostel.fr; $46bed>,
Kitchen:Y, B'fast:Y, WiFi:Y, Pvt. room:Y, Locker:Y, Desk hr:24/7;
Note: bar, lounge, near metro & Gare du Nord, terrace views, luggage ok

Caulaincourt Hostel, 2 Square Caulaincourt Paris, France;
www.*caulaincourt.com/*; T:0146064606; *bienvenue@caulaincourt.com;* $35bed>,

Kitchen:Y, B'fast:Y, WiFi:Y, Pvt. room:Y, Locker:N, Desk hr:lmtd;
Note: 2am curfew, free calls, Montmartre, few sockets, midday lock-out

Oops Hostel, 50 Ave. des Gobelins, Paris, France;
www.*oops-paris.com/*, T:0147074700, *bonjour@oops-paris.com*; $45bed>,
Kitchen:N, B'fast:Y, WiFi:Y, Pvt. room:N, Locker:N, Desk hr:24/7;
Note: midday lockout 11a>4p, left luggage, lift, a/c, free city tour

Le Regent Montmartre, 37 Blvd. de Rochechouart, Paris France;
www.leregent.com/, T:0148782400, *bonjour@leregent.com*; $48bed>,
Kitchen:Y, B'fast:Y, WiFi:$, Pvt. room:Y, Locker:N, Desk hr:24/7;
Note: left luggage, laundry, 4pm check-in, close to Metro

The Plug-Inn Hostel, 7 Rue Aristide Bruant, Paris, France;
www.plug-inn.fr/, T:0142584258, *bonjour@plug-inn.fr*; $45bed>,
Kitchen:Y, B'fast:Y, WiFi:Y, Pvt. room:Y, Locker:N, Desk hr:24/7;
Note: midday lockout, c.c. ok, left luggage, bit cramped, Montmartre

Vintage Hostel, 73 Rue Dunkerque, Paris, France; /
www.*vintage-hostel.com/*, T:0140161640, *contact@vintage-hostel.com*; $31bed>,
Kitchen:N, B'fast:Y, WiFi:Y, Pvt. room:N, Locker:Y, Desk hr:24/7;
Note: a/c, c.c. ok, travel desk, few sockets, near Gare du Nord

Absolute Hostel, 1 Rue Fontaine au Roi, Paris, France;
www.*absolute-paris.com/*, T:147004700, *bonjour@absolute-paris.com*; $35bed>,
Kitchen:N, B'fast:Y, WiFi:Y, Pvt. room:N, Locker:N, Desk hr:24/7;
Note: max. stay 15 nights, c.c. ok, cozy, lift, bike & city tours, forex

Le Montclaire Montmartre, 62 Rue Ramey, Paris, France;
www.*montclair-hostel.com/*, T:0146064607, *bonjour@lemontclair.com*; $36bed>,
Kitchen:Y, B'fast:Y, WiFi:Y, Pvt. room:Y, Locker:N, Desk hr:24/7;
Note: 6 flights of stairs, good location, left luggage

Woodstock Hostel, 48 Rue Rodier, Paris, France;
www.*woodstock.fr/*, T:0148788776, *flowers@woodstock.fr*; $38bed>,
Kitchen:Y, B'fast:Y, WiFi:Y, Pvt. room:Y, Locker:N, Desk hr:24/7;
Note: 2am curfew, left luggage, bar, linen fee, cash only, midday lockout

Aloha Hostel, 1 Rue Borromée, Paris, France;
www.*aloha.fr/*, T:0142730303, *friends@aloha.fr*; $39bed>,
Kitchen:Y, B'fast:Y, WiFi:Y, Pvt. room:N, Locker:N, Desk hr:24/7;
Note: linen fee, tour, no power in bedroom, 4p check-in, beer machine

TOULOUSE is France's fourth-largest city, a major university town and center of Europe's aerospace industry, including Airbus. It lies in the mid-Pyrenees region of southern France, so something of a capital for the Languedoc region. Its history goes back to the Roman and Merovingian eras and it withstood the northern advance of Muslim conquerors. Its medieval buildings include the Gothic cathedral of Saint-Étienne, the Romanesque basilica of Saint-Sernin, and the Gothic Église des Jacobins. *www.toulouse.world-guides.com/*

La Petite Auberge de Compostelle (St-Sernin), 17 rue d'Embarthe, Toulouse; www.*gite-compostelle-toulouse.com/*, T:0760881717; $29bed>,
Kitchen:Y, B'fast:N, WiFi:Y, Pvt room:N, Locker:Y, Desk hr:10a-9p;
Note: advise late arrival, luggage ok, noon lockout, laundry, central

9) Germany

At the beginning of the last millennium, the Holy Roman Empire was largely comprised of German territories, and their kings became Holy Roman emperors. There was always competition between Prussia and Austria, though, so no real political unity, and the religious unity was fractured with the German-based Protestant Reformation initiated by Martin Luther, from which it would never recover. Napoleon's conquests put a definitive end to the Holy Roman Empire (finally) and a German state was able to coalesce—minus Austria—in 1871 under the leadership of Otto von Bismarck. By this time Germany was a hotbed of ideas and science and literature and art and was anxious to make a name for iself. It was also landlocked and overpopulated and largely surrounded by Slavic peoples that it had little sympathy with. The results of two World Wars were disastrous.

Today Germany is the industrial heart of Europe, the engine that keeps the rest of it running and competitive, and one of the world's major export economies. It's also a major moral force, having been divided into opposite political poles and reunited successfully. The division of the country into Communist and Democratic halves set it back a hundred years, until reunification finally came in 1990. Still this is a nation that likes its R&R, and hostelling is strong ('ß' is equivalent to 'ss' btw, and pronounced as such, frequently seen in the German word "Straße"=strasse=street). Many German cities rank high in world "liveability" ratings. German is the language, Euro is the currency, and the telephone country code is +49.

www.germany.travel

BERLIN is Germany's capital and largest city and is documented from the 13th century. It was the capital of Prussia before becoming the capital of a united, then redivided, Germany. The city as well as the country was divided of course, and nothing was a better symbol of the Cold War than the isolated enclave of West Berlin struggling to survive while surrounded by Communist East Germany. With the fall of the Berlin Wall and the eventual reunification of the country (a fact which never ceases to amaze me) Berlin resumed its role as the country's undivided capital, and party central. That's *party* party, not Communist party.

Berlin is famous for its museums, including the Dahlem Museum complex in Dahlem district, the Egyptian Museum, the new National Gallery and Museum of Arts and Crafts, the Brucke-Museum, the Berlin Museum and the museum of Transport and Technology, for starters. Other landmarks include the Berlin Wall, of course, or at least what's left of it, and the controversially restored Reichstag building—Hitler's old stomping grounds. Then there are the Philharmonic Hall, the New National Gallery of modern art, the Hall for Chamber Music, the Charlottenburg Palace, St. Nicholas Church, Palace of the Republic, the Church of Mary, Town Hall, St. Hedwig's Cathedral, Brandenburg Gate, and Museum Island, with its healthy handful of monuments to knowledge. Hostels here are pretty good, but not necessarily the best. Kitchens are optional, and breakfasts will usually cost you bucks, though the many that have restaurants means that other meals are available also, not to mention beer.

www.berlin.de/

Inn-Berlin, Prinzenallee 49, Berlin, Germany;
www.*inn-berlin.de/*, T:03049301901, *info@inn-berlin.de/*; $26bed>,
Kitchen:Y, B'fast:$, WiFi:Y, Pvt. room:Y, Locker:Y, Desk hr:lmtd;
Note: parking, bike hire, forex, TV, private bath, bit distant, min. stay 2 nights

Grand Hostel Berlin, Tempelhofer Ufer 14, Berlin, Germany;
www.*grandhostel-berlin.de/*, T:03020095450; $23bed>, Kitchen:N, B'fast:$
Wi-Fi:Y, Pvt. room:Y, Locker:Y, Desk hr:24/7;
Note: no bunks, bar, café, bike hire, laundry, TV, stairs, min. stay 2 nights

EastSeven Berlin Hostel, Schwedter Strasse 7, Berlin, Germany;
www.*eastseven.de/*, T:03093622240, *info@even.de*; $24bed>,

Kitchen:Y, B'fast:$, WiFi:Y, Pvt. room:Y,
Locker:Y, Desk hr:7a>12m;
Note: c.c. ok, city tour, travel desk, left luggage, dinners, pub crawl

U Inn Berlin, Finowstrasse 36, Berlin, Germany;
www.*uinnberlinhostel.com/en*, T:03033024410,
info@uinnberlinhostel.com; $20bed>, Kitchen:Y,
B'fast:$, WiFi:Y, Pvt. room:Y, Locker:Y, Desk hr:7a>1a;
Note: left luggage, books, c.c. ok, parking, tour, safe, suburb

Baxpax Downtown Hostel, Ziegelstrasse 28, Berlin, Germany;
www.*baxpax.de/*, T:03027874880, *info@baxpax-downtown.de*; $20bed>,
Kitchen:N, B'fast:$, WiFi:Y, Pvt. room:Y, Locker:Y, Desk hr:24/7;
Note: bar, café, parking city tour, bike hire, c.c. ok, laundry, linen fee

Comebackpackers, Adalbertstrasse 97, Berlin, Germany;
www.*comebackpackers.com/*, T:03060057527; $20bed>,
Kitchen:Y, B'fast:$, WiFi:Y, Pvt. room:N, Locker:Y, Desk hr:24/7;
Note: bar, café, bikes, laundry, tours, cheap beer!

Heart of Gold Hostel, Johannisstrasse 11, Berlin, Germany;
www.*heartofgold-hostel.de/*, T:03029003300; $20bed>,
Kitchen:N, B'fast:$, WiFi:Y, Pvt. room:Y, Locker:Y, Desk hr:24/7;
Note: bar, c.c. ok, free tour, travel desk, loud

Jetpak Eco-Lodge, Pücklerstr. 54, Berlin, Germany;
www.*jetpak.de/*, T:0308325011, *city@jetpak.de*; $20bed>,
Kitchen:N, B'fast:Y, Wi-Fi:Y, Pvt. room:Y, Locker:Y, Desk hr:lmtd;
Note: in forest, close to bus, solar power, parking, left luggage

Pfefferbett Hostel, Christinenstrasse 18, Berlin, Germany;
www.*pfefferbett.de/*, T:03093935858, *info@pfefferbett.de*; $22bed>,
Kitchen:N, B'fast:$, WiFi:Y, Pvt. room:Y, Locker:Y, Desk hr:24/7;
Note: bar, restaurant, laundry, bikes, lift, c.c. ok, tour

Swimming Hostel Berlin, Zur Alten Flussbadeanstallt 5,
Berlin, Germany; www.*swimming-hostel-berlin.de/*, T:01725463760; $12bed>,

Kitchen:Y, B'fast:$, WiFi:Y, Pvt. room:Y, Locker:N, Desk hr:lmtd;
Note: parking, TV, laundry, converted barge, bit far & hard to find

Main Station Hostel, Quitzowstrasse 110, Berlin, Germany; www.*mainstationhostel.de*, T:03039409750, hostel@*mainstationhostel.de*; $17bed>, Kitchen:Y, B'fast:$, WiFi:Y, Pvt. room:Y, Locker:Y, Desk hr:24/7;
Note: bar, parking, free tour, laundry, c.c. ok, no-party hostel, modern, far

Wombats City Hostel, Alte Schönhauser St. 2, Berlin, Germany; www.*wombats-hostels.com*/, T:0308471082/0, *office@wombats-miunich.de*; $27bed>, Kitchen:Y, B'fast:$, WiFi:Y, Pvt. room:Y, Locker:Y, Desk hr:24/7;
Note: bar, café, lift, c.c. ok, laundry, rooftop bar

Three Little Pigs Hostel, Stresemannstrasse 66, Berlin, Germany; www.*three-little-pigs.com/*, T:03026395880, *info@three-little-pigs.de*; $21bed>, Kitchen:Y, B'fast:$, WiFi:Y, Pvt. room:Y, Locker:Y, Desk hr:24/7;
Note: café, bar, laundry, parking, c.c. ok, free tour, bike hire, computers

PangeaPeople Hostel, Karl-Liebknecht-Strasse 34, Berlin, Germany; www.*pangeapeople.de/*; T:030886695815; $22bed>, Kitchen:N, B'fast:N, WiFi:Y, Pvt. room:N, Locker:Y, Desk hr:24/7;
Note: bar, café, lift, tour, bikes, travel desk, no computers, central

Schlafmeile Hostel, Weichselstrasse 25, Berlin, Germany; www.*schlafmeile.de*/, T:03096514676; $16bed>, Kitchen:Y, B'fast:N, WiFi:Y, Pvt. room:Y, Locker:Y, Desk hr:lmtd;
Note: bar, café, c.c. ok, tour, bike hire

Backpacker Berlin, Knorrpromenade 10, Berlin, Germany; www.*backpackerberlin.com/*, T:03029369164, *backpackerberlin@yahoo.de*; $17bed>, Kitchen:Y, B'fast:Y, WiFi:Y, Pvt. room:Y, Locker:Y, Desk hr:8a>12m;
Note: c.c. ok, city tour, bike hire, travel desk, laundry

Helter Skelter Hostel, Kalkscheunenstrasse 4, Berlin, Germany; www.*helterskelterhostel.com/*, T:03028044997; $19bed>,

Kitchen:Y, B'fast:$, WiFi:Y, Pvt. room:Y, Locker:Y, Desk hr:24/7;
Note: bar, tour, c.c. ok, safe dep., party hostel, smoking indoors

Amstel House, Waldenserstr. 31, Berlin, Germany;
www.*amstelhouse.de/,* T:0303954072, *info@amstelhouse.de;* $20bed>,
Kitchen:N, B'fast:$, WiFi:Y, Pvt. room:Y, Locker:Y, Desk hr:24/7;
Note: bar, talking, tour, c.c. ok, laundry

Baxpax Mitte Hostel, Chausseestr. 102, Berlin, Germany;
www.*baxpax.de/,* T:+49(0)3028390965, *info@backpacker.de;* $:21>
Kitchen:Y, B'fast:N, WiFi:Y, Pvt. room:Y, Locker:Y, Desk hr:24/7;
Note: bar, tour, laundry, c.c. ok, bike rent, left luggage

CityHostel Berlin, Glinkastr. 5-7, Berlin, Germany;
www.*cityhostel-berlin.com,* T:+49(0)30238866850; $23bed>,
Kitchen:N, B'fast:Y, WiFi:Y, Pvt. room:Y, Locker:Y, Desk hr:24/7;
Note: wheelchair ok, bar, lounge, parking, beer garden, terrace, central

Plus Berlin, Warschauer Platz 6, Berlin, Germany;
www.*plushostels.com,* T:03021238501; $25bed>,
Kitchen:N, B'fast:$, WiFi:Y, Pvt. room:Y, Locker:Y, Desk hr:24/7;
Note: wheelchair ok, resto/bar, parking, free tour, lift, laundry, pool

Residenz 2000, Unter den Eichen 96, Berlin, Germany;
www.*residenz-2000.de/,* T:03081056253, *info@residenz-2000.de;* $16>,
Kitchen:Y, B'fast:$, WiFi:Y, Pvt. room:N, Locker:Y, Desk hr:7a>10p;
Note: c.c. req, lift, parking, dry cleaning, solarium, restaurant, not central

Singer109 Apartment-Hostel, Singerstrasse 109, Berlin, Germany;
www.*singer109.com/*, T:0308687870, *office@singer109.com;* $29bed>,
Kitchen:N, B'fast:$, WiFi:Y, Pvt. room:Y, Locker:Y, Desk hr:24/7;
Note: resto/bar, lift, tour desk, smoking, TV, c.c. ok, near train not central

Citystay Mitte, Rosenstrasse protest 16, Berlin, Germany;
www.*citystay-hostel.eu/,* T:03023624031, *info@citystay.de;* $18bed>,
Kitchen:N, B'fast:$, WiFi:Y, Pvt. room:Y, Locker:Y, Desk hr:24/7;
Note: bar/café, tour desk, luggage room, laundry, central

Academy Hotel, Dennewitzstrasse 7, Berlin, Germany; www.*academy-hotel.de*, T:03089049730; $32bed>, Kitchen:Y, B'fast:$, WiFi:Y, Pvt. room:Y, Locker:Y, Desk hr:8a>7p;
Note: café, parking, lift, luggage room, laundry, tour desk, c.c. ok

Globetrotter Hostel Odyssee, Grünberger Strasse 23, Berlin; www.*globetrotterhostel.de*, T:03029000081, odyssee@*globetrotterhostel.de;* $18bed>, Kitchen:Y, B'fast:$, WiFi:Y, Pvt. room:Y, Locker:Y, Desk hr:24/7;
Note: resto/bar, luggage room, laundry, tour desk, c.c. ok, central, stairs

Metropol Hostel, Mehringdamm 32, Berlin, Germany; www.*metropolhostel-berlin.com*, T:03025940890, info@*metropolhostel-berlin.com*; $18bed>, Kitchen:N, B'fast:$, WiFi:Y, Pvt. room:Y, Locker:Y, Desk hr:24/7;
Note: wheelchair ok, bar/café, tour desk, parking, lift, luggage room

Sunflower Hostel, Helsingforser Strasse 17, Berlin, Germany; www.su*nflower-hostel.de*, T:03044044250, hostel@*sunflower-hostel.de*; $18bed>, Kitchen:N, B'fast:$, WiFi:Y, Pvt. room:Y, Locker:Y, Desk hr:24/7;
Note: café, bar, bike rent, luggage room, TV, parking, c.c. ok

Hostel Die Etage East, Langhansstrasse 8, Berlin, Germany; www.*die-etage-east.de/*, T:030548190, *info@die-etage-east.de*; $16bed>, Kitchen:Y, B'fast:N, WiFi:Y, Pvt. room:Y, Locker:Y, Desk hr:lmtd;
Note: east side, wheelchair ok, parking, free tour, travel desk, luggage ok

Berlin Intl. Youth Hostel, Kluckstrasse 3, Berlin, Germany; www.*hihostels.com*, T:0302611097, *jh-berlin@jugendherberge.de*; $20bed>, Kitchen:N, B'fast:Y, WiFi:Y, Pvt. room:N, Locker:Y, Desk hr:24/7;
Note: resto/bar, parking, tour/travel desk, luggage ok, laundry, c.c. ok

Pegasus Hostel, Strasse der Pariser Kommune 35, Berlin, Germany; www.*pegasushostel.de*; T:0302977360, *hostel@pegasushostel.de*; $17bed>, Kitchen:Y, B'fast:$, WiFi:Y, Pvt. room:Y, Locker:Y, Desk hr:24/7;
Note: resto/bar/café, 5th Fl no lift, laundry, lift, parking, free tour, c.c. ok

Pension - Maximun, Lückstrasse 17, Berlin, Germany;
www.*pension-maximum.de/*, T:03085617480, *info@pension-maximum.de;*
$29bed>, Kitchen:N, B'fast:$, Wi-Fi:Y, Pvt. room:Y,
Locker:N, Desk hr:24/7;
Note: luggage room, laundry, parking, far from center close to tube, mkt

Lette'm Sleep Hostel, Lettestrasse 7, Berlin, Germany;
www.backpackers.de/berlin, T:03044733623, *info@backpackers.de;* $20bed>,
Kitchen:Y, B'fast:N, WiFi:Y, Pvt. room:Y, Locker:Y, Desk hr:lmtd;
Note: wheelchair ok, bike rent, luggage ok, tour desk, c.c. ok, coffee/tea

Smart-hostel Berlin, Genter Strasse 53, Berlin, Germany;
www.*smarthostel-berlin.de*, T:03045486454; $16bed>,
Kitchen:N, B'fast:$, WiFi:Y, Pvt. room:Y, Locker:N, Desk hr:24/7;
Note: wheelchair ok, lift, parking, luggage rm, tour desk, c.c. ok

A&O Berlin-Mitte, Köpenicker Strasse 127-129, Berlin, Germany;
www.*aohostels.com*, T:030809475200; $31bed>,
Kitchen:N, B'fast:$, WiFi:$, Pvt. room:Y, Locker:Y, Desk hr:24/7;
Note: bar, parking, tour desk, luggage room, pets ok, TV, lift

Corner Hostel, Driesener Strasse 17, Berlin, Germany;
www.*corner-hostel.de/*, T:03043734353; $21bed>,
Kitchen:Y, B'fast:$, WiFi:Y, Pvt. room:Y, Locker:Y, Desk hr:24/7;
Note: wheelchair ok, bar/café, bike rent, luggage ok, laundry, free tour

All In Hostel/Hotel, Grünberger Str. 54, Berlin, Germany;
www.*all-in-hostel.com/*; T:+49302887683; *stay@all-in-hostel.com*; $25bed>,
Kitchen:N, B'fast:$, WiFi:Y, Pvt. room:Y, Locker:Y, Desk hr:24/7;
Note: wheelchair ok, resto/bar, pet ok, lift, bike rent, free tour, laundry

Generator Hostel Berlin, Storkower Strasse 160, Berlin, Germany;
www.*generatorhostels.com*, T:0304172400,
berlin@generatorhostels.com, $23bed>, Kitchen:N, B'fast:$,
WiFi:Y, Pvt. room:Y, Locker:Y, Desk hr:24/7;
Note: wheelchair ok, resto/bar, free tour, travel desk, bike rent, c.c. ok

Design Hotel DDR, Wriezener Karree 5, Berlin, Germany; www.*ostel.eu*, T:03025768660, contact@*ostel.eu*; $20bed>, Kitchen:N, B'fast:$, WiFi:Y, Pvt. room:Y, Locker:Y, Desk hr:24/7; **Note:** bar/club, parking, luggage room

Check !N Hostel, Markgrafenstrasse 68, Berlin, Germany; www.info@*check-in-hostel.de*; T:03025923797; $9bed>, Kitchen:N, B'fast:$, WiFi:Y, Pvt. room:N, Locker:Y, Desk hr: 24/7; **Note:** wheelchair ok, resto/café, luggage room, c.c. ok, new

BREMEN is another north German Hanseatic city with much medieval history and the architecture to prove it. For tourist sights Roland, the city's mythic protector immortalized in a statue on the main plaza, sounds like the hot ticket, unless you prefer statues of the donkey, dog, cat, and rooster from the Grimm Brothers' fairy tale. The old town also includes the Gothic Town Hall, the marketplace and the 11th C. cathedral. Then there's Becks Brewery, for when the clock strikes beer:30.

www.bremen-tourism.de/

Townside Hostel, Am Dobben 62, Bremen, Germany; *www.townside.de/*, T:042178015, *info@townside.de*; $20bed>, Kitchen:Y, B'fast:$, WiFi:Y, Pvt. room:Y, Locker:Y, Desk hr:>11p; **Note:** bike rent, parking, laundry, luggage ok, special meal deals, central

Gasthaus Bremer Backpacker Hostel, Emil-Waldmann-Strasse 5, Bremen; *www.bremer-backpacker-hostel.de*, T:04212238057; $25bed>, Kitchen:Y, B'fast:$, WiFi:Y, Pvt. room:N, Locker:Y, Desk hr:lmtd; **Note:** linen fee, luggage ok, laundry, terrace, cash only, near train/center

Hostel-Posty, An der Weide 50, Bremen, Germany; *www.hostel-posty.de*, T:042133456000, *hostel-posty@live.de*; $25bed>, Kitchen:Y, B'fast:Y, WiFi:Y, Pvt. room:Y, Locker:N, Desk hr:24/7; **Note:** coffee & tea, close to train, stairs, no lift

The Grand Hostel Bremen, Feuerkuhle 30, Bremen, Germany; www.*thegrandhostel.com/*, T:04216437209, *info@thegrandhostel.com*; $20bed>,

Kitchen:Y, B'fast:$, WiFi:Y, Pvt. room:Y, Locker:Y, Desk hr:lmtd;
Note: parking, luggage room, TV, c.c. ok, linen free for 3N stay, central

COLOGNE (KOELN) is a western German trading city of the same vintage as Hamburg, Germany's fourth largest, and part of the massive Rhine-Ruhr metropolitan area which totals more than ten million. This all started as a tiny Germanic village pre-BC, and expanded in 50 AD into a Roman "Colonia" (Colonia=Cologne, get it?). It was an important trade center. The Franks took over in 459 until it became part of the Holy Roman Empire later. Napoleon occupied it briefly, and then Prussia in 1815 until the creation of the German state. Meanwhile Cologne was absorbing smaller towns and becoming heavily industrialized. Cologne was occupied by the British and French under the terms of the Versailles Treaty ending WWI, and devastated during WWII. It has since rebuilt, based less on heavy industries and more on services, insurance, and media.

Tourism is also important, with green spaces, prominent museums, fairs and festivals, and dozens of restaurants and pubs. But the entertainment is still a little tamer than Hamburg and elsewhere. The big deal here is the Carnival, which starts on 11-11 at 11:11 and continues until Ash Wednesday (?). Prominent sights include the Gothic cathedral, which is a UNESCO World Heritage site, and is the city's symbol. Other prominent churches in Romanesque style include those of Sankt Gereon, S. Severin, Ursula, Maria im Kapitol, Kunibert, Pantaleon, Aposteln, and Gross Sankt Martin. Roman remains include portions of the original wall, a banquet hall floor, remains of the North Gate and a large part of the Praetorium. Three of the original twelve gates in the medieval wall survive. Hostel quality here is better than much of Germany.

www.cologne.de/

Pathpoint Cologne, Allerheiligenstrasse 15, Cologne, Germany;
www.*pathpoint-cologne.de/en*, T:022113056860, *info@pathpoint-cologne.de*;
$28bed>, Kitchen:Y, B'fast:$, WiFi:Y, Pvt. room:Y, Locker:Y, Desk hr:24/7;
Note: c.c. ok, laundry, games, convenient, no lift

Weltempfanger Backpacker Hostel, Venloer Str. 196, Cologne;
www.*koeln-hostel.de/*, T:022199579957, *info@koeln-hostel.de/*; $25bed>,

Kitchen:Y, B'fast:$, WiFi:Y, Pvt. room:Y, Locker:Y, Desk hr:7a>12m;
Note: bar, left luggage, bikes, c.c. ok, not central, E20 key deposit

Station Hostel Backpackers, Marzellenstrasse 44, Cologne, Germany;
www.hostel-cologne.de/, T:02219125301, *station@hostel-cologne.de*; $22bed>,
Kitchen:Y, B'fast:$, WiFi:Y, Pvt. room:Y, Locker:Y, Desk hr:24/7;
Note: bar, c.c. ok, lift, laundry, close to train, smoke-friendly

Youth Hostel Cologne-Riehl, An der Schanz 14, Cologne, Gremany;
www.jugendherberge.de, T:0221976513-0, koeln-riehl@jugendherberge.de;
$37bed>, Kitchen:N, B'fast:Y, WiFi:Y, Pvt. room:Y, Locker:N, Desk hr:24/7;
Note: bar, restaurant, lift, laundry, c.c. ok, lots of students, clinically clean

A&O Koln Neumarkt, Mauritiuswall 64-66, Cologne Germany;
www.aohostels.com/en/ T:0221467064700; $29bed>,
Kitchen:N, B'fast:$, WiFi:$, Pvt. room:Y, Locker:Y, Desk hr:24/7;
Note: bar, parking c.c. ok, travel desk, linen fee, left luggage

DRESDEN is an East German cultural city, in a Saxon area with Slavic roots. Its central core received 3900 tons of incendiary bombs from 1300 UK and US heavy bombers which destroyed thirty-nine square kilometers of the city in four raids between 13-15 February, 1945. Ouch! Those bombs killed 25,000 people, an event immortalized in *Slaughterhouse Five* by Kurt Vonnegut, and still controversial to this day. Dresden became a major industrial center in Communist East Germany and Vladimir Putin was stationed there from 1985-90 as a KGB agent while the Wall fell farther north. The nearby Elbe valley is a UNESCO world heritage site for its parks and monuments. Dresden is now regaining its status as a major cultural center. Its heart is still the Rococo-style Zwinger in the old city and a cluster of Baroque churches: the Frauenkirche, the Hofkirche, and the Kreuzkirche. Besides the Zwinger museums there are the Semper Gallery and the Japanese palace. There is also the Opera House, the Dresden State Theatre, and the Dresden Philharmonic Orchestra.

www.dresden.de/

Hostel Kangaroo-Stop, Erna-Berger-Str. 8-10, Dresden, Germany;
www.kangaroo-stop.de; T:0351314345-5; info@*kangaroo-stop.de*; $16bed>,

Kitchen:Y, B'fast:$, WiFi:$, Pvt. room:Y, Locker:Y, Desk hr:24/7;
Note: bar, parking, linen fee, close to train

Hofgarten 1824, Theresienstrasse 5, Dresden, Germany;
www.hofgarten1824.de/; T:03512502828; *reservierung@hofgarten1824.de;* $22bed>, Kitchen:N, B'fast:$, WiFi:Y, Pvt. room:N, Locker:Y, Desk hr:lmtd;
Note: bar, parking, travel desk, left luggage, close to train & old town

Hostel Lollis Homestay, Görlitzer Str. 34, Dresden, Germany;
www.lollishome.de/en/; T:03518108458; *lolli@lollishome.de*; $18bed>, Kitchen:Y, B'fast:$, WiFi:Y, Pvt. room:Y, Locker:Y, Desk hr:24/7;
Note: free bikes, tea & coffee, dinners, laundry, linen fee, hippie-ish

Hostel Mondplast, Louisenstrasse 77, Dresden, Germany;
www.mondpalast.de/; T:03515634050; *info@mondpalast.de*; $21bed>, Kitchen:Y, B'fast:$, WiFi:Y, Pvt. room:Y, Locker:Y, Desk hr:24/7;
Note: bar, restaurant, c.c. ok, travel desk, close to nightlife

A&O Dresden Hauptbahnhof, Strehlener Strasse 10, Dresden;
www.aohostels.com/en/dresden/; T:03514692715900; $29bed>, Kitchen:N, B'fast:$, WiFi:$, Pvt. room:Y, Locker:Y, Desk hr:24/7;
Note: rooftop bar, parking, games, travel desk, c.c, ok, close to train

DUSSELDORF is a center of German fashion, advertising, telecommunicaitons, and… beer, *altbier*, that is, old-school, the top-fermenting pre-lager, hoppier, crisper kind: black gold, Westphalia tea. They have a lively regional competition going with Cologne, including the annual Carnival that starts on 11-11 at 11:11, etc. Landmarks in the city include the 13th–14th C. Lambertuskirche (Lambertus Church), and the old town hall, Jägerhof Castle, Benrath Castle, and remains of the palace of Frederick I (Barbarossa).

www.duesseldorf.de

A&O Dusseldorf Hbh, Corneliusstrasse 9, Dusseldorf, Germany;
www.aohostels.com; T:+49(0)21133994-4800; $43bed>, Kitchen:Y, B'fast:$, WiFi:$, Pvt. room:Y, Locker:Y, Desk hr:24/7;
Note: bar, parking, tour desk, luggage room, laundry, c.c. OK, near train

Jugendherberge Düsseldorf, Düsseldorfer St. 1, Düsseldorf, Germany; *www.duesseldorf.jugendherberge.de*; T:+49(0)211557310; $36bed>, Kitchen:N, B'fast:Y, WiFi:Y, Pvt. room:Y, Locker:Y, Desk hr:24/7;
Note: HI fee, resto/bar, luggage room, laundry, c.c. ok, tour desk

Backpackers Dusseldorf, Fürstenwall 180, Dusseldorf, Germany; *www.backpackers-germany.de;* T:02113020848; info@*backpackers-germany.de;* $26bed>, Kitchen:Y, B'fast:Y, WiFi:Y, Pvt. room:N, Locker:Y, Desk hr:>10p;
Note: luggage room, parking, TV/DVD's

FRANKFURT is not Germany's largest city, but it may be its most international. Prior to the establishment of the Holy Roman Empire, Frankfurt was little more than a shallow spot in the River Main suitable as a ford for the Franks, yep. It is notable that the Frankfurt *Messe* (Trade Fair), for which it is famous today, was mentioned as long ago as 1150. It was heavily damaged during WWII and little remains of the medieval city. Today it is Germany's fifth-largest city and the financial center of it and Europe both, home to major banks, major trade fairs and a stock exchange. It is also home to people of some 180 nationalities. Follow the money.

Notable landmarks include the city's Zoological Garden, the Stadel Art Institute and Municipal Gallery, the Senckenberg Natural History Museum, and the Liebeighaus museum of Sculpture. There is also a major red-light district near the train station, a veritable shopping center of sex, if that's your thing. You wouldn't believe how hotel prices soar during trade fairs. Since much of its tourism is of the business sort, there are only a few hostels in Frankfurt; too bad. There is a porn theater in the airport.

www.frankfurt.de/

Five Elements Hostel, Moselstrasse 40, Frankfurt, Germany; *http://5elementshostel.de,* T:06924005885, *welcome@5elementshostel.de*; $45bed>, Kitchen:Y, B'fast:$, WiFi:Y, Pvt. room:Y, Locker:Y, Desk hr:24/7;
Note: close to train, theme nights, café/bar, free tour, bike rent, lift

Frankfurt Hostel, Kaiserstrasse 74, Frankfurt, Germany; www.*frankfurt-hostel.com;* T:0692475130; *info@frankfurt-hostel.com*; $29bed>,

Kitchen:Y, B'fast:Y, WiFi:Y, Pvt. room:N, Locker:Y, Desk hr:24/7;
Note: close to train, café/bar, luggage room, laundry, lift, c.c. ok, pasta

HAMBURG sits at the base of the Jutland Peninsula where it joins Europe, strategically located with the North Sea close by to the west, and connected to Hamburg by river, and the Baltic Sea close by to the east, where its historic trading partner Lubeck is located. It is Germany's second city and a major trading port since the days of the Hanseatic League and the old Holy Roman Empire, long before the idea of a unifed Germany had even been imagined. It was a free city-state, in fact, for much of its history, and was the point from which ethnic Germans, including my ancestors, typically left for America. These days it is still a major port, Europe's second largest in fact, but tourism is a major economic factor now, also.

Hamburg has more than 2000 bridges over its numerous canals and rivers, giving it a romantic look to match its romantic setting of architecture and arts. There is an old town, too, though with little traditional architecture aside from the five churches of Sankt Jacobi, S. Petri, S. Katharinen, S. Nikolai, and S. Michaelis. Museums include the Kunsthalle, the Museum of Arts and Crafts, and the museum of Ethnoloogy and Prehistory. Seamen need their outlets and entertainment, too, of course, and Hamburg's got that, home to Europe's largest red-light district, claiming among its many residents and victims many a St. Pauli girl and the Beatles, who prepared for stardom here. Take a stroll along the *Reeperbahn* in the evening to soak up the atmosphere. Looking's free. Hamburg is home to many musicians and artists, and many a good festival. Many hostels are converted brothels; gave them an "A" for atmosphere.

http://english.hamburg.de/

Generator Hostel Hamburg, Steintorplatz 3,
Hamburg; *generatorhostels.com/*; T:040226358460; $25bed>,
Kitchen:N, B'fast:$, WiFi:Y, Pvt. room:Y, Locker:Y, Desk hr:24/7;
Note: bar, laundry, tour, c.c. ok, lift, close to train & center

A&O Hamburg Hammer Kirche, Hammer Landstr. 170, Hamburg;
www.aohostels.com/de/hamburg/; T:04064421045500; $35bed>,
Kitchen:N, B'fast:$, WiFi:$, Pvt.room:Y, Locker:Y, Desk hr:24/7;
Note: bar, parking, wheelchair ok, c.c. ok, close to metro & center

Wira Hostel, Königstrasse 16a, Hamburg, Germany;
www.wirahostel.hostel.com/, T:0407699-7202; $22bed>, Kitchen:Y, B'fast:$, WiFi:Y, Pvt. room:Y, Locker:Y, Desk hr:8a>10p;
Note: c.c. +3%, laundry, free tour, $ for extras, Thai food

Kosrtanien Hostel, Kastanienallee 27, Hamburg, Germany;
www.kastanien-hotel.net/; T:04053253364; *kontakt@kastanien-hotel.de*; $34bed>, Kitchen:N, B'fast:N, WiFi:Y, Pvt room:Y, Locker:N, Desk hr:10a>10p;
Note: bar, parking, ex-brothel, linen fee obligatory, colorful area

Kiezbude, Lincolnstrasse 2, Hamburg, North Sea Coast, Germany;
www.kiezbude.com/; T:04074214269; *kontakt@kiezbude.com*; $35bed>, Kitchen:N, B'fast:N, WiFi:Y, Pvt. room:Y, Locker:N, Desk hr:>10p;
Note: min. stay 3 nights, ex-brothel, bar, café, free tour, travel desk, hard find

HEIDELBERG is not one of Germany's largest cities, but it has certainly seen some history. The half-million-year-old (give or take a couple 100K) "Heidelberg Man" was discovered here and since his time the area has been claimed by various tribes—Celts, Romans, Germans, and Holy Romans—until the foundation of the modern German state. Heidelberg was a stronghold of the Nazi party. Now Heidelberg is best known for its university and tourism. The Castle above town is the main attraction, but the old town and bridge are nice, too. Other landmarks include the Heiliggeistkirche and the Marstall, the Knight's House, the town hall, and the Jesuitenkirche. There's an American military base here; it's moving.

www.heidelberg.de

Lotte–Backpackers Hostel Heidelberg, Burgweg 3 Heidelberg;
www.lotte-heidelberg.de, T:062217350725, info@*lotte-heidelberg.de*; $30bed>, Kitchen:Y, B'fast:N, WiFi:Y, Pvt. room:Y, Locker:Y, Desk hr:8a>10p;
Note: parking, luggage room, laundry, c.c. ok, central

Steffis Hostel Heidelberg, Alte Eppelheimer Str. 50, Heidelberg;
www.hostelheidelberg.de, T:062217782772, *stefffi@hostelheidelberg.de*; $24bed>, Kitchen:Y, B'fast:N, WiFi:Y, Pvt. room:N, Locker:Y, Desk hr:8a>10p;
Note: bar/club, parking, tour desk, luggage ok, c.c. ok, near supermarket

Sudpfanne Hostel, Hauptstraße 223, Heidelberg, Germany; *www.heidelberger-sudpfanne.de/*, T:06221163636, *info@heidelberger-sudpfanne.de;* $26bed>, Kitchen:N, B'fast:$, WiFi:Y, Pvt. room:Y, Locker:Y, Desk hr:>12m; **Note:** resto/bar, cash only, one-off linen fee, central

MUNICH is now Germany's third-largest city and the largest in Bavaria. It rates highly on liveability indices and has much less crime than Germany's largest metropli, but is also more expensive, almost in proportion to its proximity to the Alps. It dates from at least the twelfth century when it was a settlement of Benedictine monks. It derived income from a monopoly on the salt trade and grew enough to become the capital of Bavaria in the early 1500's. It soon became a center of the Counter-Reformation and brown beer. Hitler's Beer Hall Putsch in 1923 occurred here, resulting in his arrest and imprisonment. I guess they should have drunk lager. Munich was a stronghold when Hitler came to power ten years later. The Nazi's first concentration camp at Dachau was only 10mi/16km away. It suffered seventy-one air raids during the subsequent war. Since then it has focused on rebuilding and it is more than a little ironic that Israeli athletes were murdered at the Summer Olympics here in 1972.

Oktoberfest is the big deal for entertainment here, and is held annually every... September. With culinary specialties that include baked sausage loaf, pork knuckle, and *beuscherl* (look it up), the strudel-ly desserts come as something of a relief. Then there are the beer gardens and the famous *Hofbrauhaus*. *Kultfabrik* should be worth checking out. Three of the seven original 14th century town gates still stand, and other medieval buildings include the cathedral, the Frauenkirche, and the old Town Hall. Munich's oldest church, Peterskirche, has been rebuilt. Museums include the Bavarian State Picture Galleries, the Neue Pinakothek, and the Deutches Museum. Hostel quality is so-so, with kitchens optional, breakfast usually pricey, and services costing extra.

www.muenchen.de/int/en/

Wombats City Hostel, Senefelderstrasse 1, Munich, Germany; *www.wombats-hostels.com/*; T:01799484144; *office@wombats-munich.de;* $30bed>, Kitchen:N, B'fast:$, WiFi:Y, Pvt. room:Y, Locker:Y, Desk hr:24/7; **Note:** bar, parking, laundry, lift, travel desk, convenient to train, free drink

Euro Youth Hostel, Senefelderstrasse 5, Munich, Germany;
www.euro-youth-hotel.de/, T:08959908811, *info@euro-youth-hotel.de;* $25bed>,
Kitchen:N, B'fast:$, WiFi:$, Pvt. room:Y, Locker:Y, Desk hr:24/7;
Note: bar, laundry, bikes, lift, c.c.+/%, close to train, dorm age limit 35

Easy Palace City Hostel, Mozartstrasse 4, Munich, Germany;
www.easypalace.de/; T:0895587970; *info@easypalace.de;* $27bed>,
Kitchen:Y, B'fast:$, WiFi:$, Pvt. room:N, Locker:N, Desk hr:24/7;
Note: bar, prkng, laundry, c.c. ok, free tour, distant, close to Oktoberfest

Easy Palace Station Hotel, Schützenstrasse 7, Munich, Germany;
www.easypalace.de/; T:0895525210; *station@easypalace.de;* $26bed>,
Kitchen:N, B'fast:$, WiFi:$, Pvt. room:Y, Locker:N, Desk hr:24/7;
Note: bar, parking, tour, c.c. ok

The 4You Hostel Munich, Hirtenstraße 18, Munich, Germany;
www.the4you.de/, T:0895521660; $25bed>, Kitchen:N, B'fast:Y,
WiFi:Y, Pvt. room:Y, Locker:Y, Desk hr:24/7;
Note: bar, parking, tour, laundry, travel desk, convenient to train & center

STUTTGART is located in southwestern Germany in the state of Baden-Wurttemberg and historically has been home to various Germanic groups and the Frankish Merovingians. Nowadays it's best known as the home of the Mercedes-Benz. Despite the heavy industry, Stuttgart is green and ranks high in liveability, and the nearby Alps and Black Forest are tourist delights. Historic landmarks include the old castle, the Rosenstein Palace, the Gothic Leonhardskirche, and the Stiftskirche (collegiate church), a 12th C. Romanesque basilica. The Cannstatter Folk Festival is held nearby every autumn, and there are mineral springs, too.

www.stuttgart.de/

Inter-Hostel, Paulinenstrasse 16, Stuttgart, Germany;
www.inter-hostel.com/, T:071166482797, *info@inter-hostel.com;* $26bed>,
Kitchen:Y, B'fast:$, WiFi:Y, Pvt. room:N, Locker:N, Desk hr:7a>11p;
Note: laundry, parking, c.c. ok, central

10) Greece

Greece is where Europe began, specifically Western Europe, west of Egypt and Babylon and Jerusalem, at least, its most illustrious contemporaries. The Greece of classical antiquity emerged in Athens and culminated in the "Greater Greece" of Alexander the Great that stretched from Greece to Central Asia, and left Greek-speakers and Greek culture all over the world. It now lies far to the east of the major modern Western Europe population centers of London, Paris, and Rome. Still western it is, with traditions of language, philosophy, science, and government that were tried, tested, and transmitted directly to Rome and elsewhere over two thousand years ago. After then being dominated by Rome it eventually entered into a sort of partnership, with the "new Rome" of the Eastern (Byzantine) Roman Empire established at Constantinople, Greek of speech, culture and religion. For over 1000 years it was one of history's greatest empires.

Constantinople fell to the Ottoman Turks in 1453 and the rest of Greece fell soon thereafter, only regaining independence in 1830, minus Constantinople (Istanbul). Politics since then have been a roller-coaster of leftists and rightists battling for the hearts and minds of the people in a never-ending struggle. Only in religion and alphabet is Greece perhaps closer to the Slavic Eastern Europe of which it is a contiguous part, and which barely existed in the classical age, within the region at least. Greece has little to do with former master and eastern neighbor Turkey, and largely defines itself that way. Still it is connected to them all by road, boat and plane. Tourism is a mainstay of the economy, and Greece has no less than seventeen UNESCO World Heritage Sites. Aside from the classical sites, Greece is best known for its islands, many of which are party central for gap-year kids with the means to get there. They along with Thessaloniki and Athens constitute the touristic Athens. Greek is the language. The phone code is +30. The currency is Euro; wait a minute...

www.visitgreece.gr/

ATHENS is where Western civilization began, with accomplishments in philosophy, politics, art, and literature that are unsurpassed to this day. Athens is also one of the world's oldest cities, documented from 1400 BC, when it played a role in the preclassical Mycenaean culture, and today the largest city and capital of Greece. After centuries of neglect as a part of the Ottoman Empire, Athens today has returned to much of its previous vitality and importance. It has also overcome much of its horrendous smog problem of a few decades ago, and today is fairly pleasant, especially in the tourist areas under the Parthenon. Piraeus is the major port and is only a short train ride away. It resembles nothing so much as a modern airport with ferries coming and going constantly. As always the main problem in Athens is the economy.

The main tourist sights center on the ancient Acropolis and its crown jewel, the Parthenon. Then there is the National Archeological Museum. Those expecting an eastern Rome-like "museum city" full of medieval art and architecture will be disappointed. During the civil war Athens was mostly depopulated and destroyed. Only the Plaka below the Acropolis maintains some of that ambience, with streets devoted to certain crafts and other vestiges of that era. Still the Acropolis is not the only classical site of interest. There is also the Roman-built Odeum theatre built in 161 AD and now used in the summer festival of music and drama, and the Theatre of Dionysius to which it is attached. Others are found in the Agora, including the Theseum, a 5th Century BC temple. Then there are the 42-foot-high Horologium water clock and the Byzantine church Aylos Eleftherios.

www.breathtakingathens.com/

Athens Backpackers, 12 Makri St, Makryanni, Athens, Greece;
www.backpackers.gr/, T:**+302109224044;** *info@backpackers.gr*; $29bed>,
Kitchen:Y, B'fast:Y, WiFi:Y, Pvt. room:Y, Locker:Y, Desk hr:24/7;
Note: bar, café, a/c, c.c. ok, laundry, luggage room, parking, travel desk

Athens Studios, 12 Makri St, Makrigianni, Athens, Greece; *www.athensstudios.gr/*, T:**+302109235811,** *info@athensstudios.gr*; $33bed>, Kitchen:Y, B'fast:Y, WiFi:Y, Pvt. room:Y, Locker:N, Desk hr:8a>12m; **Note:** bar, luggage ok, laundry, lift, a/c, c.c. ok, good location, roof view

AthenStyle, Agias Theklas, No 10, Athens, Greece; *www.athenstyle.com/*, T:+302103225010, *info@athenstyle.com;* $26bed>, Kitchen:Y, B'fast:Y, WiFi:Y, Pvt. room:Y, Locker:Y, Desk hr:24/7; **Note:** bar, laundry, a/c, c.c. ok, location, rooftop bar

Student & Travelers Inn, 16 Kydathineon, Plaka, Athens, Greece; *www.studenttravellersinn.com/*, T:2103248802, *info@studenttravellersinn.com;* $24bed>, Kitchen:N, B'fast:$, WiFi:Y, Pvt. room:Y, Locker:N, Desk hr:24/7; **Note:** bar, café, laundry, luggage room, cold, few outlets, good location

Hotel Fivos, 23 Athinas St, Monastiraki, Athens, Greece; *www.hotelfivos.gr/en/*, T:+302103226657; $13bed>, Kitchen:N, B'fast:Y, WiFi:Y, Pvt. room:Y, Locker:N, Desk hr:24/7; **Note:** bar, travel desk, a/c, c.c. ok, central, outside noise

Hostel Zorba's, 10 Gkyilfordou St., Victoria Square, Athens, Greece; *www.zorbashotel.com/*, T:2108224927, *info@zorbashotel.com*; $14bed>, Kitchen:N, B'fast:$, WiFi:Y, Pvt. room:Y, Locker:Y, Desk hr:24/7; **Note:** c.c.+5%, bar, laundry, luggage room, a/c, colorful area

Neo Olympos Hotel, 38 Theodorou Diligianni St, Athens, Greece; *www.hotelneosolympos.com/*, T:2106223433, *info@hotelneosolympos.com;* $13bed>, Kitchen:N, B'fast:Y, WiFi:Y, Pvt. room:Y, Locker:Y, Desk hr:24/7; **Note:** luggage room, a/c, c.c. ok, close to metro but not sights

Pagration Hostel, 75 Damareos St, Athens, Greece; *www.athens-yhostel.com/*, T:+302107519530, *y-hostels@otenet.gr*; $16bed>, Kitchen:Y, B'fast:N, WiFi:Y, Pvt. room:Y, Locker:N, Desk hr:24/7; **Note:** laundry, non-tourist area, pay for shower

Athens Intl YH, Viktoros Ougko 16, Metaxourgio, Greece; *www.athens-international.com/*, T:2105232540, *info@athens-international.com;*

$13bed>, Kitchen:N, B'fast:$, WiFi:Y, Pvt. room:Y, Locker:Y, Desk hr:24/7;
Note: max. stay 7 nights, laundry, lift, a/c, left luggage, colorful neighborhood

Athens Easy Access, Satovriandou 26, Athens, Greece;
www.athenseasyaccess.com/, T:+302105243211; $22bed>,
Kitchen:N, B'fast:Y, WiFi:Y, Pvt. room:Y, Locker:N, Desk hr:24/7;
Note: bar, laundry, lift, a/c, c.c. ok, free tour, not best neighborhood

CORFU is one of Greece's best-known islands. Lying off the northwest coast, it is as close to Albania as it is to Greece, and centuries of domination by Italy and Britain make it culturally more European than most of Greece. Its location on the ferry run from Italy to Greece, back during Communism when that was the only international surface route, also has made it a staple on Western tourist circuits. Many of the hostels are self-contained compounds, I suppose so that you can get shit-faced and not have to worry how to get home. Of course if you only do that, then you'll miss much of the rich history of Corfu, which was part of the Venetian republic for many years and still carries vestiges of that era. That makes it different from the rest of Greece and highly worth a look around. The Royal Palace, once the residence of British governors and now a museum, survived the destruction of WWII.
www.corfu-tourism.com/

Pink Palace, Agios Gordios Beach, Sinarades, Corfu I., Greece;
www.thepinkpalace.com/, T:2661053025, *info@thepinkpalace.com*; $30bed>,
Kitchen:N, B'fast:Y, WiFi:Y, Pvt. room:Y, Locker:Y, Desk hr:24/7;
Note: bar, club, a/c, c.c. ok, activities, parties, compound atmosphere

Sunrock Backpackers', Sunrock (Vrachos), Pelekas Beach, Sinarades;
www.sunrockcorfu.com/, T:+302661094637, *sunrock77@gmail.com*; $24bed>,
Kitchen:N, B'fast:Y, WiFi:$, Pvt. room:Y, Locker:N, Desk hr:24/7;
Note: free dinner, arpt. pick-up, isolated, family-run, beach

Corfu Backpackers' Inn, Agios Gordios Beach, Corfu Island, Greece;
www.corfubackpackers.com/, T:6945230727, *info@corfubackpackers.com*; $22bed>,
Kitchen:N, B'fast:Y, WiFi:N, Pvt. room:Y, Locker:N, Desk hr:24/7;
Note: free dinner & arpt.pickup, resto-bar, club, pool, activities

CRETE is the largest and most populous of the Greek Islands and is in fact a center of Greek culture more ancient than Athens itself. The Minoan culture here flourished at more or less the same time as that of ancient Egypt, and to this day Crete still has a culture distinctively its own. Minoan sites are found at Knossos, Phaestus, and elsewhere on the island. There is an Archeological Museum in Heraclion, the capital city.

http://explorecrete.com/

Rethymno Youth Hostel, 41 Tobazi St, Rethymno, Crete Island; *www.yhrethymno.com/,* T:+302831022848, *info@yhrethymno.com*; $14bed>, Kitchen:Y, B'fast:$, WiFi:Y, Pvt. room:N, Locker:N, Desk hr:8a>11p;
Note: few sockets, close to everything, bar

Youth Hostel Plakias, Mirthios, Rethymno, Crete Island; *www.yhplakias.com/,* T:+302832032118; $13bed>,
Kitchen:N, B'fast:$, WiFi:Y, Pvt. room:N, Locker:N, Desk hr:lmtd;
Note: min. stay 2 nights Apr-Oct, bar, parking, luggage ok, far from town/beach

IOS ISLAND is part of the Cyclades Group in the Aegean. It has developed a bit since its hippie days of a few decades ago. Today Chora is a picturesque town of boutiques and bars, and the beaches are open for business. The archeological site of Skarkos dates back to the Cyclades culture which was the first advanced culture of Greece.

www.greeka.com

Far Out Beach Club, Mylopotas Beach, Ios Island, Greece; *www.faroutclub.com/,* T:302286092305, *village@faroutclub.com*; $13bed>, Kitchen:N, B'fast:$, WiFi:Y, Pvt. room:Y, Locker:N, Desk hr:24/7;
Note: bar, restaurant, pool, laundry, forex, close to beach, bus to town

Markos Village, Chora, Ios Island, Greece; *www.markosvillage.com/,* T:+302286091059, *george@markosvillage.com*; $14bed>, Kitchen:N, B'fast:$, WiFi:Y, Pvt. room:Y, Locker:Y, Desk hr:24/7;
Note: resto-bar, club, a/c, c.c. ok, parking, balconies, walk to town

Purple Pig Stars, Mylopotas Beach, Ios Island, Greece; *www.purplepigstars.com/*, T:2286091302, *info@purplepigstars.com*; $13bed>, Kitchen:Y, B'fast:N, WiFi:Y, Pvt. room:Y, Locker:N, Desk hr:lmtd; **Note:** resto-bar, laundry, pool, a/c, c.c. ok, parking, travel desk, on beach

MYKONOS ISLAND is a major tourist destination. Attractions include 16th century windmills, the medieval Church of Paraportiani, the Square of Three Wells, and, of course, lots of water. It is the point of departure for the sacred island of Delos. There is air service to Athens and boat connections to elsewhere in the Cyclades Group of islands.

www.mykonos.gr

Paraga Beach Hostel, Mykonos Camping, Paraga Beach, Mykonos Island; *http://paragabeachhostel.com/*, T:22890-25915, *info@mycamp.gr*; $13bed>, Kitchen:Y, B'fast:$, WiFi:Y, Pvt. room:Y, Locker:Y, Desk hr:24/7; **Note:** free arpt. pick-up, bar, restaurant, pool, laundry, forex, c.c. ok, basic

PAROS ISLAND has abandoned marble quarries and mines and is well-connected to Piraeus with several ferries per day. There are many villages, but Parikia is the main town, with an archeological museum and an ancient Christian church. The Parian Chronicle, which recounts artistic milestones in ancient t Greece, was found here in1627.

http://paros-travel.com/

Ampeli Studios Apts., Paros Island, Parikia, Paros Island; *http://ampeli-studios-paros.a1hostels.com/*, T:6939089289, *info@ampelistudios.com;* $17bed>, Kitchen:Y, B'fast:N, WiFi:Y, Pvt. room:Y, Locker:Y, Desk hr:lmtd; **Note:** luggage room, laundry, central, a/c, c.c. ok, on beach, port pick-up

SANTORINI ISLAND is also in the Cyclades group, the remains of a huge volcano that erupted and whose caldera then sunk below the water, leaving an island ring around a large lagoon. The beaches have much black sand, the color dependent on the geologic layer exposed. Wear sandals. The climate is a desert one.

www.travel-to-santorini.com/

Anny Studios, Perissa Beach, Santorini Island, Greece;
www.annystudios.com/, T:2286031626, *hotelanny@sanforthnet.gr*; $20bed>,
Kitchen:Y, B'fast:$, WiFi:Y, Pvt. room:Y, Locker:N, Desk hr:lmtd;
Note: bar, pool, forex, laundry, travel desk, a/c, beach near, far from town

Katerina & John Hotel, Perissa, Santorini Island, Greece;
www.matrix-santorini.com/, T:2286082833, *cheaphotelperissa@gmail.com*; $9bed>,
Kitchen:N, B'fast:N, WiFi:Y, Pvt. room:Y, Locker:N, Desk hr: 24/7;
Note: ferry shuttle, parking, pool, a/c, c.c. ok, luggage room, scooter rent

THESSALONIKI is Greece's second city, as it was long ago in the Byzantine Era as "co-capital" with Constantinople. If Athens was the cultural capital of ancient Greece, then Thessaloniki is the cultural capital of the modern one. Equal parts Greek, Balkan, Anatolian and Mediterranean, it has always stood along the border of cultures mixing and mingling as circumstances demanded, be it ancient Macedonians, Illyrians, Thracians, and Slavs, or modern Turks, Jews, Muslims, Slavs, and...oh yeah, Greeks. There are transport links in all directions. Thessaloniki was also an important early Christian center. Paul wrote First Thessalonians here. In the 9th century Greek missionaries Cyril and brother what's-his-name methodically standardized the Old Church Slavonic language, the first literary language for Slavs. There are many Byzantine churches still standing, including the Ayia Sofia, the church of Ayia Dimitrios, the Panaghia Chalkeon, and the church of Osios David. Today it has a rep as a party town. Have fun.

www.saloniki.org/

Little Big House, Andokidou 24, Thessaloniki, Greece;
www.littlebighouse.gr/, T:2313014323, *contact@littlebighouse.gr*; $22bed>,
Kitchen:Y, B'fast:$, WiFi:Y, Pvt. room:Y, Locker:Y, Desk hr:lmtd;
Note: free coffee/tea, luggage room, travel desk, c.c. ok, near old city

RentRooms, Konstantinou Melenikou 9, Thessaloniki, Greece;
www.rentrooms-thessaloniki.com/, T:2310204080,
info@rentrooms-thessaloniki.com; $24bed>, Kitchen:N, B'fast:Y,
WiFi:Y, Pvt. room:Y, Locker:Y, Desk hr:lmtd;
Note: resto/bar, café, bike rent, a/c, luggage room

Studios Arabas, Sachtouri 28, Ano Poli, Thessaloniki, Greece; *www.hostelthessaloniki.com,* T:306973817188, *pappas3kala@gmail.com;* $16bed>, Kitchen:Y, B'fast:N, WiFi:Y, Pvt. room:Y, Locker:N, Desk hr:lmtd; **Note:** a/c, laundry, travel desk, tea & coffee, hard to find, steep climb

Pension Tzitzifies,Agiou Dimitriou-Oikon-Agia Triada-Dimos Thermaikou; *www.pension-tzitzifies.gr/,* T:+306932336127, *linaras@otenet.gr;* $18bed>, Kitchen:Y, B'fast:N, WiFi:Y, Pvt. room:Y, Locker:N, Desk hr:lmtd; **Note:** next to PLAZ EOT, min. stay 3 nights, advise arrival time, parking, beach

Hotel Rex, 39 Monastiriou St., Thessaloniki, Greece; *www.rexhotelthessaloniki.gr/,* T:+302310517051, *info@rexhotelthessaloniki.gr;* $25bed>, Kitchen:N, B'fast:Y, WiFi:Y, Pvt. room:Y, Locker:N, Desk hr:24/7; **Note:** gay friendly, luggage room, laundry, forex, travel desk, near train

11) Iceland

Iceland was settled by Norsemen in the ninth century AD, but there is good reason to think that Irish monks had already been there. The fact that the Norse apparently took Gaelic slaves (and maybe wives) there would make genomic evidence inconclusive. It belonged first to Norway, then to Denmark, before gaining independence in 1944. Today it is home to over 300,000 people, most of whom have traditionally made their living from the sea. That all changed in the early years of the current millennium when Iceland got the brilliant idea to become a financial center, with all the shenanigans that advanced capitalism is famous for. That was a disaster, of course, and Iceland is still recovering, a terrible shame for a country with a reputation as having one of the lowest income disparities in the world.

On a lighter note, the pop music is some of the best in the world—Bjork, Sigur Ros, and all the rest. The language is closer to Old Norse than any modern Scandinavian language. The main source of energy is geothermal and the island is full of volcanoes and geysers. The northern tip of the island kisses the Arctic Circle. There is a road that rings the island, which I figure would make an excellent two-three day car-camping tour under the summer's midnight sun. Icelandic Air has some of the cheapest flights between Europe and the East Coast of the US. They'll let you stopover at no extra charge for three days. Icelandic is the language; *krona* (ISK) is currency; phone code is +354.

REYKJAVIK is the capital and largest (read: "only") city in Iceland. It was founded in 870, but didn't develop much as a city until the 18th century. Like its sister Nordic cities on the mainland, it is quite attractive, though much smaller. It's expensive, too, the cheapest fast food around $10 USD and any sit-down meal easily $25. There are at least a hundred bars; they close at 4:30 a.m. on weekends, so the sun's already rising in summer. The Reykjavík Art Museum and the Sigurjón Ólafsson Museum are among the town's many museums and galleries. Hostels are good quality, albeit typically with linen fees (sleeping bags usually OK).

www.visitreykjavik.is

Reykjavik Downtown Hostel, Vesturgata 17, Reykjavik, Iceland; *www.hostel.is/*, T:5538120, *reykjavikdowntown@hostel.is*; $36bed>, Kitchen:Y, B'fast:$, WiFi:Y, Pvt. room:Y, Locker:N, Desk hr:24/7;
Note: linen fee, luggage ok, prkng, travel desk, c.c. ok, member discount

Kex Hostel, Skúlagata, 101 Reykjavik, Iceland; *www.kexhostel.is/*, T:5616060, *info@kexhostel.is*; $25bed>, Kitchen:Y, B'fast:$, WiFi:Y, Pvt. room:Y, Locker:N, Desk hr:24/7;
Note: resto/bar, laundry, luggage room, c.c. OK, linen fee

Aurora Guesthouse, Freyjugata 24, Reykjavik, Iceland; *www.aurorahouse.is/*, T:3548991773, *book@aurorahouse.is*; $32bed>, Kitchen:Y, B'fast:N, WiFi:Y, Pvt. room:Y, Locker:N, Desk hr:24/7;
Note: laundry, travel desk, c.c. ok, close to center & bus

Reykjavik Backpackers, Laugavegur 28, Reykjavik, Iceland; *www.reykjavikbackpackers.is/*, T:578-3700, *bookings@reykjavikbackpackers.is*; $27bed>, Kitchen:Y, B'fast:$, WiFi:Y, Pvt. room:Y, Locker:$, Desk hr:24/7;
Note: bar, laundry, luggage, travel desk, c.c. ok

Domus Guesthouse, Hverfisgotu 45, Reykjavik, Iceland; *www.domusguesthouse.is/*, T:+354561-1200, *domus@simnet.is*; $31bed>, Kitchen:N, B'fast:$, WiFi:Y, Pvt. room:N, Locker:N, Desk hr:lmtd;
Note: parking, free laundry, luggage room, high linen fee, good location

12) Ireland

Like Great Britain, Ireland was connected by land to the continent of Europe when sea levels were lower and ice covered the land. There is evidence of agriculture here from 4000 BC and Bronze and Iron Age artifacts that indicate trade with the other Celtic countries of Britain and the continent. By the time of the Roman Empire, Ireland was thoroughly settled by Gaelic Celts. The Roman presence itself here was not significant, except for the Christian missionaries that came in the last days of Empire, especially Saint Patrick in 432 AD. Thus was established a nation and culture of monks and saints and Roman scholars far superior to what remained in the Europe of Dark Age turbulence and migrations. Roman culture persisted in Ireland hundreds of years after it had been rendered asunder elsewhere, because of its very isolation.

So when Charlemagne and his regime wanted to revive the Roman Empire on the Continent, they needed the learned men of Ireland to help them. Vikings caused havoc in the ninth century, but their cousins the Frenchified Normans came to conquer and stay. Ultimately they did more staying than conquering, assimilating into the population despite efforts to prevent it. The English didn't get serious about conquering until the 17th century, and within a couple hundred years it was complete. Ireland joined the UK in 1801 and almost immediately started trying to undo it. Where Scotland, already purged of Catholics, benefited greatly from that union, for Ireland it was the opposite. "Plantations" of English and Scots were unjust, as were laws favoring Protestants, as was famine in 1840.

By then many people just wanted to leave. So they did, decimating a population that hasn't risen to that level again as of this day. The Industrial Revolution didn't help much, either. That was elsewhere. The rise of nationalism gave freedom to Ireland by 1920, minus Ulster. At least it spared Ireland the Nazi bombings. It wasn't until toward the end of the 20th century as Ireland joined the EU that things started looking better. Membership has its privileges. We're still waiting final fallout from the Great Depression of 2008. Ireland has had some of the greatest writers of the English language while being the last bastion of the Irish language. Euro is currency. Phone code is +353.

www.discoverireland.com/ca-en/

CORK is in the far south of the island and is Ireland's second largest city. It is a city of culture and industry, considering itself as distinct from the rest of Ireland, the "Rebel County." Back in the early days of English aggression, it was one of their few outposts outside of Dublin, definitely "beyond the Pale." English residents in Cork used to pay "Black Rent" to the surrounding Gaels, for protection, from the surrounding Gaels. That sounds fair. Its famous producta are Murphy's Irish Stout and Viagra. Culture is to be found in the Crawford municipal art gallery, the Cork Opera House, the Triskel arts centre, the Cork Public Museum, and many art galleries. The city is also home to the long-established Guinness Jazz Festival. Landmarks are the Protestant cathedral of St. Fin Barre and the Roman Catholic St. Mary's Cathedral. There is a covered market.

www.cork-guide.ie/

Bru Bar & Hostel, 57 MacCurtain St, Cork, Co. Cork, Ireland;
www.bruhostel.com/, T:0214501074, *info@bruhostel.com*; $20bed>,
Kitchen:Y, B'fast:Y, WiFi:Y, Pvt. room:N, Locker:N, Desk hr:24/7;
Note: bar, TV, tour desk, luggage room, laundry, c.c. ok, near bus/center

Sheilas Hostel, 4 Belgrave Place, Wellington Road, Cork, Ireland;
www.sheilashostel.ie, **T:+353(0)214505562,** *info@sheilashostel.ie*; $17bed>,
Kitchen:Y, B'fast:$, WiFi:Y, Pvt. room:Y, Locker:N, Desk hr:24/7;
Note: restaurant, sauna, laundry, tour desk, forex, c.c. ok, near bus, uphill

Kinlay House Cork, Bob and Joan's Walk, Shandon, Cork City, Ireland; *www.kinlayhousecork.ie/*, T:0214508966, *info@kinlayhousecork.ie*; $20bed>, Kitchen:Y, B'fast:Y, WiFi:Y, Pvt. room:Y, Locker:N, Desk hr:24/7; **Note:** luggage room, laundry, forex, c.c. ok, good location

Cork International Hostel, 1 Red Cliff, Western Rd, Cork, Ireland; *http://anoige.ie/*, T:0214543289, *info@anoige.ie*; $16bed>, Kitchen:Y, B'fast:$, WiFi:Y, Pvt. room:Y, Locker:N, Desk hr:lmtd; **Note:** member discount, restaurant, luggage ok, c.c. ok, call after 5pm

DUBLIN is Ireland's capital and largest city. It was originally a Viking settlement, Celts not being especially citified, apparently. Normans were largely assimilated, and the city grew rapidly until union with the UK in 1801, when it stagnated and declined. Dublin Castle was the English stronghold since 1204, but their dominion was gradually reduced in size until it included not much more than Dublin. English domination was defined by a wooden perimeter called the "Pale." Beyond the Pale the country was still Irish. 1801 changed all that, as innovation and trade largely shifted to English-dominated Belfast. Dublin Castle is the premier landmark of Dublin, with Norse, Norman, and Georgian influences. Near it are Christ Church and St. Patrick's, both allowed to run down before being rebuilt in the 1800's. Ironically some of the finest monumental buildings stand on the north riverbank, as do the city's poorest parts. Ireland's national theatre, the Abbey, is just east of O'Connell Street.

Today Dublin is a "Celtic tiger" on a good day, its fate large tied to Europe as a whole at this point. Literarily, it is unmatched in the world, with writers like Joyce, Swift, Yeats, Shaw, Beckett and Wilde in its history. Theatre and art aren't bad, either, including "underground" genres. Music is both traditional and modern, so that means string bands and U2. It is also one of the prime party centers of Europe. This is the center of the pub culture which has been spread throughout much of the world, along with its great beers: Guiness, Murphy's, Watney's, and all the rest. Hostels are generally good quality and tend to be in and around the Temple Bar area, Dublin's medieval district, the better for drinking, I reckon.

www.visitdublin.com/

The Times Hostel-College St., 8 College St., Ranelagh, Dublin 2, Ireland; *www.timeshostels.com/*, T:016729028, college@timeshostels.com; $20bed>,

Kitchen:Y, B'fast:Y, WiFi:Y, Pvt. room:Y, Locker:N, Desk hr:24/7;
Note: luggage ok, pub crawl, laundry, c.c. ok, by Temple Bar so loud

Generator Hostel-Dublin, Smithfield Square, Dublin 7, Ireland;
www.generatorhostels.com/, T:019010222, *dublin@generatorhostels.com*, $23bed>,
Kitchen:N, B'fast:Y, WiFi:Y, Pvt. room:Y, Locker:Y, Desk hr:24/7;
Note: high towel & breakfast chg, bar, free left luggage, club, "like a hotel"

Kinlay Holuse-Dublin, 2-12 Lord Edward St, Temple Bar, Dublin 2;
www.kinlaydublin.ie/, T:016796644, info@kinlaydublin.ie; $19bed>,
Kitchen:Y, B'fast:Y, WiFi:Y, Pvt. room:Y, Locker:N, Desk hr:24/7;
Note: free city tour, bar, c.c.ok, forex, TV, tour desk, beer garden

Times Hostels-Camden Place, 8 Camden Pl, Dublin 2, Ireland;
www.timeshostels.com/, T:014758588, *amden@timeshostels.com*; $20bed>,
Kitchen:Y, B'fast:Y, WiFi:Y, Pvt. room:Y, Locker:N, Desk hr:24/7;
Note: c.c. ok, laundry, arpt shuttle, left luggage ok, fireplace, hugs, bit far

Abraham House, 83 Lower Gardiner St. I.F.S.C., Dublin 1, Ireland;
www.abraham-house.ie/, T:018550600, *stay@abraham-house.ie*; $20bed>,
Kitchen:Y, B'fast:Y, WiFi:Y, Pvt. room:Y, Locker:N, Desk hr:24/7;
Note: arpt bus stop, big place, central to transport, left luggage

Ashfield House-City Centre, 20 D'Olier St. 2, Dublin, Ireland;
www.ashfieldhouse.ie/, T:016797734, *ashfield@indigo.ie*; $13bed>,
Kitchen:Y, B'fast:Y, WiFi:Y, Pvt. room:Y, Locker:N, Desk hr:24/7;
Note: free ear plugs, cold in winter, c.c. ok, left luggage

Oliver St. John Gogarty, 21 Anglesea St, Ranelagh, D2, Ireland;
www.gogartys.ie/, T:016711822, *info@gogartys.ie*; $20bed>,
Kitchen:Y, B'fast:Y, WiFi:Y, Pvt. room:Y, Locker:Y, Desk hr:24/7;
Note: bar & club, laundry, tour desk, good location=noisy

Abigail's Hostel, 7-9 Aston Quay, Dublin 2, Ireland;
www.abigailshostel.com/, T:016779007, *stay@abigailshostel.com*; $24bed>,
Kitchen:Y, B'fast:Y, WiFi:Y, Pvt. room:Y, Locker:N, Desk hr:24/7;
Note: c.c. ok, Temple Bar area, noisy, elevator

Barnacles Temple Bar House, 19 Temple Lane S., Rathmines, Dublin 2; *www.barnacles.ie/*, T:016716277, *templebar@barnacles.ie*; $27bed>, Kitchen:Y, B'fast:Y, WiFi:Y, Pvt. room:Y, Locker:Y, Desk hr:24/7; **Note:** coast-to-coast tour to Galway, reading lights, Temple Bar area

Sky Backpackers-The Liffey, 2-4 Litton Lane, Dublin 1, Ireland; *www.skybackpackers.com/*, 018728389; $13bed>, Kitchen:Y, B'fast:Y, WiFi:Y, Pvt. room:Y, Locker:N, Desk hr:24/7; **Note:** free city tour, c.c. ok, close to Temple Bar

GALWAY is on the west coast of Ireland and has a reputation as its cultural heart. As such its percentage of Irish-language speakers is higher than elsewhere, around ten percent. Traditional music is big here, too. There are many festivals, Galway Arts Festival in July first and foremost among them. Portions of the old city walls remain. Historical architecture includes the remains of a Franciscan friary and St. Nicholas's Church, which dates from 1320.

www.galwaytourist.com/

Sleepzone, Bothar na mBan, Galway, Ireland; *www.sleepzone.ie/*, T:+353(0)91566999, *info@sleepzone.ie*; $20bed>, Kitchen:Y, B'fast:N, WiFi:Y, Pvt. room:Y, Locker:Y, Desk hr:24/7; **Note:** wheelchairs ok, lift, tour desk, luggage ok, forex, c.c. ok, central

Woodquay Hostel, 23/24 Woodquay, Galway, Ireland; *http://woodquayhostel.ie*, T:+353(0)91562618; $24bed>, Kitchen:Y, B'fast:N, WiFi:Y, Pvt. room:Y, Locker:N, Desk hr:24/7; **Note:** cash only, laundry, luggage room, parking, central, tea & coffee

KILLARNEY is one of the oldest tourist destinations in Ireland, dating to 1750, and the "ring of Kerry" is the main attraction, a 100-plus mile tour of local scenery, which has several variations on the basic theme that can be driven, biked, or hiked. Its first settlement was a monastery mid-first millennium at nearby Aghadoe, and the Normans built Parkavonear Castle there, also. Killarney was strongly Republican in the Irish War of Independence, and atrocities occurred nearby. It's better now. The town rocks in summer. Killarney Summerfest is especially nice, with major musical acts.

www.kllarney.ie

Neptune's Town Hostel, New St., Killarney, Ireland;
www.neptuneshostel.com, T:0646635255, *neptunes@eircom.net*; $19bed>,
Kitchen:Y, B'fast:Y, WiFi:Y, Pvt. room:Y, Locker:Y, Desk hr:lmtd;
Note: wheelchairs ok, luggage room, laundry, tour desk, forex, c.c. ok

Paddy's Palace Killarney, 31 New St, Killarney, Ireland;
www.paddyspalace.com; T:06435382; $11bed>,
Kitchen:Y, B'fast:Y, WiFi:Y, Pvt. room:Y, Locker:N, Desk hr:>8p;
Note: central, street parking free, close to Natl. Park

The Railway Hostel, Dennehy's Rd, Fair Hill, Killarney, Co. Kerry, Eire;
www.killarneyhostel.com, T:064635299, *info@killarneyhostel.com*; $15bed>,
Kitchen:Y, B'fast:Y, WiFi:Y, Pvt. room:Y, Locker:N, Desk hr:24/7;
Note: by train/bus, wheelchairs ok, luggage ok, laundry, tour desk, prkng

Killarney Intl. An Oige, Aghadoe House, Fossa, Killarney, Ireland;
http://anoige.ie/, T:+353(0)646631240, *info@anoige.ie*; $24bed>,
Kitchen:Y, B'fast:$, WiFi:Y, Pvt. room:Y, Locker:N, Desk hr:8a>9p;
Note: restaurant, laundry, tour desk, c.c. ok, bikes, not central, by big park

KILKENNY is only 60mi/100km south of Dublin, so an easy getaway to experience Ireland's more traditional culture. With Norman and monastic roots, these days Irish music and pub culture are main attractions. Arts and crafts are abundant and there are many festivals, such as the Rhythm and Roots Festival in May and the Arts festival in August. Kilkenny Castle is refurbished and open to view. Other historical landmarks are St. Canice's Cathedral, the Roman Catholic Cathedral of St. Mary, the churches of St. Mary and St. John, The Tholsel, Shee's Almshouse, and Grace's Old Castle. Kilkenny Ale is brewed here.

www.kilkennycity.ie/eng/vv

Kilkenny Tourist Hostel, 35 Parliament St, Kilkenny, Ireland; *www.kilkennyhostel.ie/*, T:(056)7763541, *info@kilkennyhostel.ie*; $20bed>, Kitchen:Y, B'fast:N, WiFi:Y, Pvt. room:N, Locker:Y, Desk hr:lmtd; **Note:** laundry, luggage room, safe deposit, central

Lanigan's Hostel, Rose Inn Street, Kilkenny, Ireland; *www.hostelkilkenny.ie/*, T:(0)567721718, *info@hostelkilkenny.ie*; $21bed>, Kitchen:Y, B'fast:$, WiFi:Y, Pvt. room:Y, Locker:Y, Desk hr:24/7; **Note:** resto/bar, wheelchairs ok, luggage room, laundry, a/c, c.c. ok

13) Italy

Italy is arguably the oldest country of Europe proper, inheritor to much of the culture of ancient Greece. As such it carries a lot of historical baggage, so Italy tends to chug along in the slow lane in terms of change and innovation. Still few countries can claim such a place of importance in both remote history and the modern world, China being the other obvious exception. Proto-Italy in the early years of the Common Era controlled much of the ancient known world from its base in Rome, and is one of the world's dozen largest economies in the modern one. Its maritime republics in Venice, Genoa, and elsewhere helped bring Europe out of the Middle Ages and launch the Age of Discovery. The Renaissance happened in Florence first. The lines that divide Europe into three parts—Latin, German, and Slavic—all converge on and around the borders of Italy. Then there's the line that divides past from present. It still runs well north of Sicily.

For the traveler it's both eye candy and mental floss, and its status as a top tourist draw is a mixed blessing. While the high-rollers may wax nostalgic over their candlelight dinners and their instant friends in the countryside, the budget travelers have cause for concern. For one thing, hostels are hardly of the highest quality here and websites funky or non-existent. More importantly, short-changing seems to be the national sport. Other guides won't tell you that. I will; and I don't say it lightly. You've been warned. Think you'll learn Italian language to avoid those problems? Ha! Better avoid tourist sites, too. Euro is the currency. Telephone country code is +39. *www.italia.it/en/home.html*

BOLOGNA was founded by Celts then Eruscans. Almost a reluctant Roman colony, it fared well after the fall, opening the world's first university in 1088. Always radical politically, it abolished feudal serfdom and even allowed women to study at the university level. More recently the Italian resistance was based here in WWII and the Communist Party of Italy in the 1970's. The city maintains a medieval feel, highlighted by the (leaning) "two towers" of Asinelli and Garisenda. Notable palaces of the era are the Palazzi Comunale, Podesta', Mercanzia, Re Enzio, and Palazzo Bevilacqua. Churches include S. Petronio, S. Domenico, S. Pietro, Sta. Maria del Servi, and S. Stefano. If you want to cross northern Italy from east to west, change trains here.

www.bolognawelcome.com/

Hostel Due Torri San Sisto, Via Viadagola 5, Bologna, Italy; *www.hihostels.com*, T:+39051501810, *bologna@aighostels.com*; $24bed>, Kitchen:N, B'fast:Y, WiFi:Y, Pvt. room:Y, Locker:Y, Desk hr:24/7;
Note: wheelchairs ok, parking, midday lockout, laundry, c.c. ok, no sign

FLORENCE (Firenze) is where you go when you've grown tired of Rome. If Rome is the political capital of Italy, then Florence is the cultural capital. Much of the Renaissance happened right here, in the Florence of Dante and Petrarch, Leonardo and Michelangelo, Macchiavelli and the Medici. Here sits the highest ratio of art to audience in the world. The Florentine dialect is the standard for Italian. Catch it on a warm day in the off-season, and you just might think you've died and gone to heaven. The entire city is a UNESCO world heritage site. Everything is of tourist interest, e.g. the Palazzo Vecchio, the Loggia del Lanzi, the Uffizi, the Duomo, the Medici Palace, the Strozzi Palace, the Pitti Palace, the Boboli Gardens, and much more. Florence is still a center of craftsmanship, with guilds dating back to the Middle Ages, the Ponte Vecchio (old Bridge) being one of the traditional markets for goldsmiths and jewelers. Then there's the sublime Tuscan countryside. Hostel quality is pretty good.

www.visitflorence.com/

Academy Hostel, Via Ricasoli, 9, Stairs B, 1st Fl, Florence, Tuscany; *www.academyhostel.eu/*, T:0552398665, *info@academyhostel.eu*; $41bed>,

Kitchen:Y, B'fast:Y, WiFi:Y, Pvt. room:Y, Locker:Y, Desk hr:24/7;
Note: quiet, no bunks, noon lockout, wheelchair ok, luggage ok, laundry

Ostello Gallo D'Oro, Via Cavour, 104 Florence;
www.ostellogallodoro.it/, T:0555522964, *info@ostellogallodoro.com;* $38bed>,
Kitchen:Y, B'fast:Y, WiFi:Y, Pvt. room:Y, Locker:Y, Desk hr:24/7;
Note: wheelchair ok, lift, bar, tour desk, luggage room, laundry, c.c. ok

Ostello del Chianti, V. Roma 137, Tavarnelle Val di Pesa, Firenze;
www.ostellodelchianti.it/, T:0558050265, *ostello@ostellodelchianti.it;* $21bed>,
Kitchen:N, B'fast:$, WiFi:Y, Pvt. room:Y, Locker:Y, Desk hr:lmtd;
Note: HI affiliated, 15mi/23 km south, wheelchair ok, luggage ok, parking

Florence Youth Hostel, Via della Condotta, 4 Florence, Italy;
www.florence-youth-hostel.com, T:3293980218, *florenceyouthostel@gmail.com;*
$39bed>, Kitchen:N, B'fast:N, WiFi:Y, Pvt. room:Y, Locker:N, Desk hr:>10p;
Note: non-party, lockout 10-14, advise late arrival, luggage ok, tour desk

Locanda Daniel, Via Nazionale, 22, Firenze, Italy;
www.locandadaniel.it/, T:+39055211293; $36bed>,
Kitchen:Y, B'fast:N, WiFi:Y, Pvt. room:Y, Locker:N, Desk hr:24/7;
Note: no bunks, call check-in, luggage ok, laundry, tour desk, a/c, cc ok

Emerald Palace, Via Dell' Ariento 2, Florence, Tuscany, Italy;
www.emeraldpalace.hostel.com/, T:+393291862260; $38bed>,
Kitchen:Y, B'fast:$, WiFi:Y, Pvt. room:Y, Locker:Y, Desk hr:lmtd;
Note: 2 locations, noon lockout, resto/café, tour desk, laundry, TV, a/c

David Inn, Via Ricasoli 31, Florence, Italy;
www.davidinn.it/, T:+39055213707; $33bed>,
Kitchen:Y, B'fast:N, WiFi:Y, Pvt. room:N, Locker:N, Desk hr:9a>12m;
Note: hard to find, cash only, b.y.o. towels, luggage room, tour desk

Plus Florence, Via S Caterina D'Alessandria15, Florence, Tuscany;
www.plushostels.com/, T:0556286347; $25bed>,
Kitchen:N, B'fast:$, WiFi:Y, Pvt. room:Y, Locker:Y, Desk hr:24/7;
Note: resto/bar/café, wheelchair ok, lift, pool, sauna, gym, ATM, a/c, c.c.

The Queen's, Via C. Cavour, 15, Florence, Tuscany, Italy;
www.thequeens.hostel.com/, T:+393207048921; $22bed>,
Kitchen:Y, B'fast:N, WiFi:Y, Pvt. room:Y, Locker:N, Desk hr:lmtd;
Note: advise arrival time, lockout 11a>1p, tour desk, c.c. ok, near supermkt

Hostel Santa Monaca, Via Sta. Monaca 6, Florence, Italy;
www.ostellosantamonaca.com/en/, T:055268338,
info@ostellosantamonaca.com; $24bed>,
Kitchen:Y, B'fast:N, WiFi:Y, Pvt. room:N, Locker:Y, Desk hr:lmtd;
Note: hard to find, noon lockout, luggage ok, TV, bike rent, forex, c.c. ok

MILAN was settled by Celts and served a term as capital of the Western Roman Empire between 286 and 402, before rising to international prominence in the same pre-Renaissance wave that also elevated London and Paris. These days it's the business and financial center of Italy and best known for its fashion industry and its major trade fairs. Milan is the crossroads for this region, with direct connections to most of the major countries of Europe—Spain, France, Switzerland, etc.—and of course, the rest of Italy. The Swiss border at Chiasso is only a day trip away, but almost like another dimension. Tourist sights include paintings by Leonardo and Raphael and the Gothic Milan Cathedral. The Duomo is the third largest church of Europe and a fine example of Gothic architecture. The Pinacoteca di Brera is one of the largest art galleries in Italy, and the Teatro alla Scala is one of the great theatres of the world. Many hostels here are up to modern European standards and expectations, not just cheap hotels with dorms.

www.turismo.milano.it

The Monastery Hostel, Via Bertoni, 3, Milano, Italy;
www.themonasteryhostel.it, T:0265560201, info@*themonasteryhostel.it*; $30bed>,
Kitchen:Y, B'fast:Y, WiFi:Y, Pvt. room:Y, Locker:Y, Desk hr:24/7;
Note: towel fee, lift, TV, travel desk, luggage room, landry, a/c, c.c. ok

Ciao Bella Milan, Via Giuseppe Balzaretti 4, Milan, Italy;
www.ciaobellamilan.hostel.com/, T:+39 0223951135; $28bed>,
Kitchen:Y, B'fast:Y, WiFi:Y, Pvt. room:N, Locker:Y, Desk hr:9a>12m;
Note: late breakfast, linen charge, age limit 40, 11a>2p lockout, cash only

Ostello Olinda, Via Ippocrate, 45, Milan, Italy;
www.olinda.org/, T:0264445219, ostello@olinda.org; $25bed>,
Kitchen:Y, B'fast:N, WiFi:Y, Pvt room:Y, Locker:Y, Desk hr:10a>8p;
Note: wheelchair ok, resto/bar, parking luggage room, laundry, TV, far

Hotel Kennedy, Viale Tunisia 6, Milan, Italy;
www.kennedyhotel.it/, T:0229400934, *info@kennedyhotel.it*; $32bed>,
Kitchen:N, B'fast:N, WiFi:Y, Pvt. room:Y, Locker:N, Desk hr:24/7;
Note: no computers, good location, cc+8%, bar, tour desk, c.c. ok

Hotel San Tomaso, Viale Tunisia 6, Milan, Italy;
www.hotelsantomaso.com/, T:0229514747, *hotelsantomaso@tin.it*; $36bed>,
Kitchen:N, B'fast:$, WiFi:N, Pvt. room:Y, Locker:N, Desk hr:24/7;
Note: bar, lounge, luggage room, cc+5%, central

Hotel Central Station, Via Giovanni B. Sammartini 15, Milan, Italy;
www.hotelcentralstation.com/, T:0267071766, *info@hotelcentralstation.com;*
$40bed>, Kitchen:N, B'fast:N, WiFi:Y, Pvt. room:Y, Locker:N, Desk hr:24/7;
Note: 5-day cancel, good for arpt trans and train, noise

Zebra Hostel, viale Regina Margherita 9, Milan, Italy;
www.zebrahostel.it/, T:0236705185, *zebrahostel@aruba.it*; $26bed>,
Kitchen:Y, B'fast:Y, WiFi:Y, Pvt. room:N, Locker:Y, Desk hr:24/7;
Note: wheelchair ok, bar/club, parking, luggage ok, a/c, c.c. ok, towel fee

Bed & Bed Milan, Via Ripamonti, 126, 20141 Milan, Italy;
www.bedinmilano.com/, T:025394216, *info@bedinmilano.com*; $19bed>,
Kitchen:N, B'fast:N, WiFi:Y, Pvt. room:Y, Locker:N, Desk hr:24/7;
Note: c.c. ok, not central

Hostel 3, Via Ignazio Ciaia 5, Milan, Italy;
www.hostel3.it/, T:0239820435, *info@hostel3.it*; $19bed>,
Kitchen:N, B'fast:$, WiFi:Y, Pvt. room:Y, Locker:N, Desk hr:24/7;
Note: bar, balcony, luggage room, c.c. ok, far from center

Hotel Galla, Via Privata Galla Placidia, 5, Milan, Italy;
www.hotelgalla.it/, T:0239561321, info@*hotelgalla.it/*; $28bed>,

Kitchen:N, B'fast:N, WiFi:N, Pvt. room:Y, Locker:N, Desk hr:24/7;
Note: luggage room, c.c. ok, far from center, close to train

Hostel Mr. Mido, Via Carlo Goldoni, 84, Milan;
www.hostelmistermido.com/, T:0239443510, *info@hostelmistermido.com;* $15bed>,
Kitchen:Y, B'fast:$, WiFi:Y, Pvt. room:Y, Locker:N, Desk hr:lmtd;
Note: bar, free tour, ATM, luggage room, laundry, TV, c.c. ok

Hostel HI Piero Rotta, Via Salmoiraghi 1, 20148 Milan, Italy;
www.hostelmilan.org/, T:0239267095, *milano@aighostels.com*; $28bed>,
Kitchen:N, B'fast:Y, WiFi:Y, Pvt. room:Y, Locker:Y, Desk hr:24/7;
Note: HI fee, strict cancellation policy, lockout 0930-1500

NAPLES (Napoli) is another part of Italy and another part of Europe, the most southern part: more old-fashioned, maybe a bit grimier, maybe a bit cheaper, and maybe even friendlier, so that's not all a bad thing. Naples was still speaking Greek when Rome was speaking Latin, and was a major point of diffusion for Greek culture into the Latin. The post-Roman medieval enemies in these parts were Arabs, Norman Sicilians and Ottomans. The historic center is one of Europe's largest and is a UNESCO world heritage site. If that's not enough there's another world right below it of catacombs, mines, and geothermal springs. Sights include nearby Mt. Vesuvius and the ruined city of Pompeii. Everything Neapolitan comes from here, and so does pizza. Naples has its own Duomo, a Castel Nuovo, a Royal Palace, and the National Archeological Museum, as well as the National Museum and Gallery of Capodimonte. Hostels here get generally good marks, and quality seems better than the main tourist markets up north.

www.comune.napoli.it

Hostel Giovanni's Home, Via Sapienza, 43, Naples, Italy;
www.giovannishome.com/, T:08119565641, *info@giovannishome.com*; $23bed>,
Kitchen:Y, B'fast:N, WiFi:Y, Pvt. room:N, Locker:N, Desk hr:8a>12m;
Note: 2 night min. stay, cash only, luggage ok, laundry, tour desk, a/c, c.c. ok

Hostel of the Sun, Via Guglielmo Melisurgo 15, Naples, Italy;
www.hostelnapoli.com/, T:+390814206393, *info@hostelnapoli.com;* $24bed>,

Kitchen:Y, B'fast:Y, WiFi:Y, Pvt. room:Y, Locker:Y, Desk hr:24/7;
Note: close to ferry & bus, towel fee, luggage room, tour desk, a/c, c.c. OK

Robby's House B&B, Via San Nicola dei Caserti #5, Naples, Italy;
www.robbyshouse.com/, T:+39081454546, *robbyshouse@libero.it*; $21bed>,
Kitchen:N, B'fast:Y, WiFi:N, Pvt. room:Y, Locker:N, Desk hr:24/7;
Note: laundry, luggage room

La Controra Hostel, Piazzetta Trinità alla Cesarea 231, Naples;
www.lacontrora.com/, T:+390815494014, *info@lacontrora.com*; $19bed>,
Kitchen:N, B'fast:Y, WiFi:Y, Pvt. room:N, Locker:Y, Desk hr:24/7;
Note: wheelchair ok, bar/café, towel/Internet fee, tour desk, lift, parking

6 Small Rooms, Via Diodato Lioy 18, Naples, Italy;
www.6smallrooms.com/, T:0817901378, *info@6smallrooms.com*; $24bed>,
Kitchen:Y, B'fast:Y, WiFi:Y, Pvt. room:Y, Locker:Y, Desk hr:8a>12m;
Note: central, cat, lots of stairs, luggage room, laundry, TV, c.c. ok

Hostel Mancini, Via P. S. Mancini 33, Napoli, Italy;
www.hostelpensionemancini.com/, T:0815536731,
info@hostelpensionemancini.com; $24bed>,
Kitchen:Y, B'fast:Y, WiFi:Y, Pvt. room:Y, Locker:Y, Desk hr:24/7;
Note: close to train, luggage ok, lift, tour desk, TV, forex, parking, c.c. ok

Fabric Hostel & Club, Via Bellucci Sessa 22, Portici Naples, Italy;
www.fabric-hostel.ory.it/, T:+390817765874,
ristfradiavolo@gmail.com; $20bed>,
Kitchen:Y, B'fast:$, WiFi:Y, Pvt. room:Y, Locker:Y, Desk hr:8a-2a;
Note: not central, resto/bar, towel fee, wheelchair ok, a/c, c.c. ok

Welcome Inn Hostel, Via Santa Teresa degli Scalzi, 8 Naples;
www.welcomeinn.it, T:+3908119579762, info@welcomeinn.it; $20bed>,
Kitchen:Y, B'fast:Y, WiFi:Y, Pvt. room:Y, Locker:N, Desk hr:24/7;
Note: daily programs, resto/bar, tour desk, luggage room, a/c, c.c. ok

Hostel & Hotel Bella Capri, Via Guglielmo Melisurgo 4, Naples;
www.bellacapri.it/, T:+390815529265, *info@bellacapri.it*; $21bed>,

Kitchen:Y, B'fast:Y, WiFi:Y, Pvt. room:Y, Locker:Y, Desk hr:24/7;
Note: bar, tour desk, forex, stairs, by port, luggage ok, laundry, a/c, c.c. ok

Art Hostel, Vico Luperano 7, Naples, Italy;
www.arthostel.org/; T:+3908119572400; $20bed>,
Kitchen:N, B'fast:Y, WiFi:Y, Pvt. room:Y, Locker:N, Desk hr:lmtd;
Note: restaurant, tour desk, luggage ok, hard to find, good location, a/c

Naples Pizza Hostel, Via San Paolo ai Tribunali 44, Naples, Italy;
www.naplespizzahostel.com, T:08119323562, *info@naplespizzahostel.com;*
$23bed>, Kitchen:Y, B'fast:Y, WiFi:Y, Pvt. room:Y, Locker:N, Desk hr:24/7;
Note: advise arrival time, luggage room, laundry, c.c. ok, central

AIG Hostel Mergellina, Via Salita della Grotta, Naples, Italy;
www.aighostels.com/, T:0817612346, *napoli@aighostels.com;* $19bed>,
Kitchen:N, B'fast:Y, WiFi:Y, Pvt. room:Y, Locker:Y, Desk hr:24/7;
Note: restaurant, parking, luggage room, laundry, c.c. ok, towel fee

PISA was a Roman port and after the fall managed to fend off the Lombards, Arabs, and Franks well enough to emerge as a major naval power at the turn of the last millennium, behind only Venice and Genoa. It is on the west coast half-way between Rome and Milan or Turin, so a convenient stop-over point for travelers. In addition to its famous leaning tower, and favorite son Galileo, the entire city is something of a museum in its own right, like much of Italy. Got religion? There are the notable old churches of San Pierino, San Frediano, San Sepolcro, San Nicola, San Francesco, Santa Catarina, and others. There are also medieval and Renaissance palaces.

www.italyguides.it

Hostel Pisa Tower, Via Piave, 4 Pisa, Italy;
www.hostelpisatower.it, T:+390505202454, *info@hostelpisatower.it;* $26bed>,
Kitchen:N, B'fast:Y, WiFi:Y, Pvt. room:Y, Locker:Y, Desk hr:2p-1a;
Note: midday lockout, café, bike rent, tour desk, laundry, towel/luggage fee

A Casa Doina Tower, Largo del Parlascio, 10-56127 Pisa, Italy;
www.bbacasadoina.it/, T:3891671184, *tower@bbacasadoina.it;* $33bed>,

Kitchen:Y, B'fast:N, Wi-Fi:Y, Pvt. room:Y, Locker:N, Desk hr:lmtd;
Note: cash only, advise arrival time, a/c, parking, balcony, tower views

Walking Street Hostel, Corso Italia, 58-56125 Pisa, Italy;
www.walkingstreethostel.com/, T:3930648737, *infopisahostel@gmail.com;* $29bed>,
Kitchen:Y, B'fast:N, WiFi:Y, Pvt. Room:N, Locker:Y, Desk hr:lmtd;
Note: café, parking, wheelchairs ok, tour desk, ATM, TV, a/c, c.c. ok

RIMINI was the home of Federico Fellini and is the quintessential modern Adriatic beach town. You don't come here looking for culture and history, though there is plenty here. You come here looking for fun. The beach, which has been privately claimed and developed into mini-estates, has got to be seen to be believed. During the summer the city provides bar-hop buses (or so I hear) so very civilized. Rimini is the jumping-off point to visit the independent Republic of San Marino, too. Besides the beach, there are the Roman ruins at the Arch of Augustus, the Roman bridge and the Malatesta Temple. It gets crowded in high season.

www.riminiturismo.it/

Jammin' Party Hostel, Viale Derna, 22 Rimini, Italy;
www.hosteljammin.com, T:0541390800, *info@hosteljammin.com;* $21bed>,
Kitchen:Y, B'fast:Y, WiFi:Y, Pvt. room:Y, Locker:Y, Desk hr:24/7;
Note: dorm age 17-45, bar/club, wheelchair ok, luggage ok, a/c, c.c. ok

Sunflower Beach Backpacker Hostel, Viale Siracusa, 25, Rimini;
www.sunflowerhostel.com, T:0541373432, *info@sunflowerhostel.com;* $20bed>,
Kitchen:Y, B'fast:Y, WiFi:Y, Pvt. room:Y, Locker:Y, Desk hr:24/7;
Note: café/resto/bar/club, free tour, tour desk, luggage ok, forex, c.c. ok

ROME (Roma) is frequently called "the eternal city." I don't know about that, but certainly it has stood at the crossroads of history for more than 2000 years, as the capital of the Kingdom, the Republic, and then the Empire. That all came tumbling down in 476, but the tradition carried on through the Middle Ages with Rome as the seat of the Catholic Church, and popes as the heads of state instead of emperors. In the 19th century, secular Rome became the capital of the new united Italian republic. The sights are too many to mention. Unlike most cities where landmarks are generally divided between churches and museums, here we have the added categories of castles and fountains, plazas and steps. Everything either dates before 400 or after 1400. For a thousand years or more, almost nothing was built and Rome's population dropped from as much as a million to as little as 20,000.

The Colosseum is the main reminder of the Classic Age, but aside from that and the Pantheon and the Roman Forum, the Renaissance era comprises most of what you see, including the Spanish Steps, Trevi Fountain, St. Peter's Basilica, and much much more, such as the Sant'Angelo Bridge and Castel Sant'Angelo, the Church of San Girolamo degli Schiavoni, the Palazzo Farnese, The Lateran Palace, the Tempietto, etc. Even so, it's not so huge, and very walkable. Summer can get crowded. In fact Rome gets so many tourists that it's hard to be a hostel purist. Standards here aren't as high as northern Europe. Persevere, and book far in advance.

www.rome.info/

Dreaming Rome Hostel, Via Cuma n°2, Roma, Italy;
www.dreamingromehostel.com; T:+393403916423; $39bed>,
Kitchen:Y, B'fast:Y, WiFi:Y, Pvt. room:Y, Locker:Y, Desk hr:24/7;
Note: converted flat, lift, luggage ok, laundry, tour desk, terrace, 2N min.

Lodi Hotel, Via Oristano 14, Rome, Italy;
www.lodihotelrome.com, T:+39067014643; $33bed>,
Kitchen:N, B'fast:Y, WiFi:Y, Pvt. room:Y, Locker:Y, Desk hr:24/7;
Note: café, parking, luggage ok, bit distant, cash only, dorm age limit 50

Twin Cities Rome Hostel, Viale Leonardo da Vinci, 223 Rome
www.twincitieshostel.it/, T:+393349491461, *info@twincitieshostel.it*; $25bed>,
Kitchen:Y, B'fast:N, WiFi:Y, Pvt. room:Y, Locker:Y, Desk hr:>12m;
Note: not central, advise arrival time, luggage ok, restaurant, 2N min

Litus Roma Hostel, Lungomare P. Toscanelli 186, Rome, Italy;
www.litusroma.com/, T:065697275, *info@litusroma.com*; $36bed>, Kitchen:N,
B'fast:Y WiFi:Y, Pvt. room:Y, Locker:N, Desk hr:24/7;
Note: bar, parking, tour desk, laundry, luggage room, on beach near arpt.

Funny Palace, Via Varese 33, Roma, Italia;
www.funnyhostel.com/, T:+390644703523, *info@funnyhostel.com;* $39bed>,
Kitchen:Y, B'fast:Y, WiFi:Y, Pvt. room:Y, Locker:Y, Desk hr:>11p;
Note: cash, luggage ok, advise late arrival, near Termini

Pop Inn Hostel, Via Marsala 80, Roma, Italy;
www.popinnhostel.com/, T:3483073735, *info@popinnhostel.com;* $38bed>,
Kitchen:N, B'fast:Y WiFi:$, Pvt. room:Y, Locker:Y, Desk hr:24/7;
Note: café, lift, TV, luggage room, tour desk, a/c

Hostel Alessandro Downtown, Via Carlo Cattaneo 23, Rome;
www.hostelsalessandro.com/, T:0644340147, *info@hostelsalessandro.com;* $32bed>,
Kitchen:N, B'fast:Y, WiFi:$, Pvt. room:N, Locker:Y, Desk hr:24/7;
Note: 2 free hr net, HI chg, lift, TV, tour desk, luggage ok, laundry

Hotel Beautiful 2, Via Milazzo 14, Ground Floor, Rome, Italy;
www.hotelbeautiful.net, T:0644703927, *Solomonhotels@gmail.com;* $35bed>,
Kitchen:N, B'fast:Y, WiFi:Y, Pvt. room:Y, Locker:Y, Desk hr:24/7;
Note: lift, tour desk, laundry, luggage storage, close to Termini station

Conte House Roma, Via Merulana, No. 191 Roma;
www.contehouse.com/, T:+390670453886, *info@contehouse.com;* $39bed>,
Kitchen:Y, B'fast:Y, WiFi:Y, Pvt. room:Y, Locker:N, Desk hr:24/7;
Note: advise arrival time, lift, tour desk, parking, a/c, c.c. ok, luggage ok

The Yellow, Via Palestro, 44 Rome, Italy;
www.yellowhostel.com, T:0649382682, *questions@the-yellow.com,* $40bed>,
Kitchen:N, B'fast:$, WiFi:Y, Pvt. room:Y, Locker:Y, Desk hr:24/7;
Note: resto/bar, luggage ok, tour desk, forex, c.c. ok, near Termini, party

Ares Rooms, Via Domenichino 7, Rome, Italy;
www.aresrooms.com, T:064744525, *info@aresrooms.com;* $40bed>,
Kitchen:N, B'fast:Y, WiFi:Y, Pvt. room:Y, Locker:N, Desk hr:24/7;
Note: luggage room, c.c. , tour desk, safe deposit, lift to 5th Fl, central

Mosaic Hostel, Via Cernaia 39, Rome, Italy;
www.hostelmosaic.com, T:0698937179, *info@hostelmosaic.com;* $45bed>,

Kitchen:N, B'fast:Y, WiFi:Y, Pvt. room:Y, Locker:Y, Desk hr:24/7;
Note: lift, luggage room, a/c, c.c. ok, close to Termini

Legends Hostel, Via Curtatone 12, Rome, Italy;
www.legendshostel.com/, T:0683393297, *info@legendshostel.com;* $41bed>,
Kitchen:N, B'fast:Y, WiFi:Y, Pvt. room:Y, Locker:Y, Desk hr: 24/7;
Note: lockout 10a>3p, age 18-40, café, lift, few sockets, laundry, a/c, c.c. ok

Plus Camping Roma, Via Aurelia 831 (km 8, 2), Rome, Italy;
www.plushostels.com, T:+39066623018; $24bed>,
Kitchen:N, B'fast:$, WiFi:Y, Pvt. room:Y, Locker:N, Desk hr:7a>11p;
Note: hour to city, resto/bar/club, pool, tour desk, a/c, c.c. ok, arpt transfer

Carlito's Way Hotel and Hostel, Via Villafranca 10, Rome, Italy;
www.rome-hotel-carlitosway.com, T:064440384,
info@rome-hotel-carlitosway.com; $32bed>,
Kitchen:N, B'fast:$, WiFi:Y, Pvt. room:Y, Locker:Y, Desk hr:24/7;
Note: age limit 35, 3 bldgs, bar, tour desk, luggage room, safe deposit, a/c

Freedom Traveller Hostel, Via Gaeta, 23, Rome, Italy;
www@freedom-traveller.it, T:0648913910, *info@freedom-traveller.it;* $33bed>,
Kitchen:Y, B'fast:N, WiFi:Y, Pvt. room:Y, Locker:Y, Desk hr:24/7;
Note: restaurant, tour desk, luggage room, lift, a/c, c.c. ok, central

Rome City Hostel, Viale Ippocrate 91, Rome, Italy;
www.romecityhostel.com/, T:0644362722, *info@romecityhostel.com;* $31bed>,
Kitchen:Y, B'fast:Y, WiFi:Y, Pvt. room:Y, Locker:Y, Desk hr:24/7;
Note: wheelchair ok, luggage room, a/c, c.c. ok

Ottaviano Hostel, Via Ottaviano 6, Rome, Italy;
www.pensioneottaviano.com, T:0639738138,
info@*pensioneottaviano.com;* $30bed>,
Kitchen:N, B'fast:N, WiFi:Y, Pvt. room:N, Locker:Y, Desk hr:7a>10p;
Note: cash, dorm age 13-40, tour desk, TV/DVD, no bunks, lockout noon

Hostel des Artistes, Via Villafranca, 20, Rome, Italy;
www.hostelrome.com/, T:064454365, *info@hostelrome.com;* $26bed>,

Kitchen:N, B'fast:$, WiFi:Y, Pvt. room:Y, Locker:Y, Desk hr:24/7;
B bar, tour desk, luggage room, dorm age >36, no bunks, roof garden

Youth Station Hostel, Via Livorno 5, Rome, Italy;
www.youthstation.it/, T:0644292471, *info@youthstation.it;* $32bed>,
Kitchen:Y, B'fast:N, WiFi:Y, Pvt. room:Y, Locker:Y, Desk hr: 24/7;
Note: age limit 30, tour desk, a/c, happy hour, theme nights, not central

SORRENTO is a small tourist town and ferry port on the Bay of Naples. It shares much of the same history as Naples. Holy Week festivities are one of the main attractions. There is a cathedral, the 14th century cloister of St. Frances of Assissi, and the Correale di Terranova Museum.

www.sorrentotourism.com

Seven Hostel, Via Iommella Grande, 99, Sant'Agnello Naples;
www.sevenhostel.com, T:0818786758, reservations*@sevenhostel.com;* $36bed>,
Kitchen:Y, B'fast:Y, WiFi:Y, Pvt. room:Y, Locker:Y, Desk hr:24/7;
Note: rooftop resto/bar, tour desk, laundry, forex, c.c. ok, a/c, not central

Ulisse Deluxe Hostel, Via del Mare 22, Sorrento, Italy;
www.ulissedeluxe.com/, T:0818774753, *info@ulissedeluxe.com;* $33bed>,
Kitchen:N, B'fast:$, WiFi:Y, Pvt. room:Y, Locker:N, Desk hr:24/7;
Note: bar, parking, wheelchairs ok, parking, a/c, c.c. ok, gym, central

Ostello Le Sirene, Via degli Aranci, 160, Sorrento, Naples, Italy;
www.hostellesirene.com, T:0818072925, *info@hostellesirene.com;* $24bed>,
Kitchen:Y, B'fast:Y, WiFi:Y, Pvt. room:Y, Locker:N, Desk hr:24/7;
Note: cash only, bar, tour desk, laundry, central to bus & train

TURIN (TORINO) is another of those places rich in culture and history, yet barely on the tourist map of Italy, even though it was the site of the winter Olympics in 2006. Torino has it all—industry, natural beauty, art, history—but few tourists yet. It is the home of Fiat and the shroud of Turin, housed in the Santa Sindone Chapel of the cathedral of San Goiovanni Batista. Other notable churches include La Consolata and the basilica of Superga, the royal burial church. Palaces include the Madama Palace, the Carignano Palace, and the Royal Palace. There is a Museum of Antiquities, an Egyptian Museum, and a Gallery of Modern Art. East-west trains pass through; it's worth a stop.

www.turismotorino.org/index.aspx

Hostel TO, Via Modane 17, Turin, Italy;
www.hostel.to, T:+39011331176, *info@hostel.to;* $24bed>, Kitchen:N, B'fast:N, WiFi:Y, Pvt. room:N, Locker:Y, Desk hr:lmtd;
Note: luggage room, c.c. ok, garden, not central

Ostello Campidoglio, Via Corio 11, Torino;
www.hotelcampidoglio.it, T:0117765808, *info@hotelcampidoglio.it;* $28bed>, Kitchen:N, B'fast:Y, WiFi:Y, Pvt. room:Y, Locker:N, Desk hr:8a>3p;
Note: wheelchair ok, resto/bar, c.c. ok, Sat TV, central

VENICE (Venezia) inherited much of the power and prestige that once belonged to Rome, via the post-Roman capital at Ravenna and by alliance with the Eastern Empire at Constantinople. Soon it morphed from a set of lagoons to a city-state to an independent empire of its own based on naval power in the Adriatic Sea. So it was going strong back in the Middle Ages, when most of the rest of Europe was just beginning to wake up after a long cultural snooze. Back then Venice was distribution point for the Silk Road and staging ground for the Crusades. Famous nowadays for its canals (connecting 118 islands) and romantic atmosphere, for many Venice embodies the essence of Europe. For others—travelers and locals, too—it's a bit too much, with one of the highest tourist-to-locals ratios in the world. Tourist attractions include the Grand Canal, St. Mark's Basilica, the Molo, the Doge's Palace, the Campanile, the Old Library, and the Piazza San Marco. Hostels are expensive and the quality is fair to middling.

www.italyguides.it

Holiday Center, Il Lato Azzurro, via Forti, 13, S.Erasmo Venezia;
www.latoazzurro.it, T:(0039)0415230642, *info@latoazzurro.it;* $41bed>, Kitchen:N, B'fast:Y, WiFi:Y, Pvt. room:Y, Locker:N, Desk hr:lmtd;
Note: resto/bar, bikes, luggage ok, laundry, ATM, pet ok, rural island

San Geremia Rooms, campo San Geremia 290, Venice, Italy;
www.hotelsangeremia.com, T:041716245, *sangeremia@yahoo.it;* $33bed>,
Kitchen:N, B'fast:N, WiFi:Y, Pvt. room:Y, Locker:N, Desk hr:lmtd;
Note: 0100 curfew, dorm age limit 35, cash only, lockout midday, no lift

Alloggi Gerotto Calderan, Campo San Geremia, Italy;
www.casagerottocalderan.com/, T:041715562, *info@casagerottocalderan.com;*
$33bed>, Kitchen:N, B'fast:N, WiFi:Y, Pvt. room:Y, Locker:N, Desk hr:lmtd;
Note: cash only, 0100 curfew, close to train, dorm age limit 35, 2 bldgs

Hotel/Hostel Colombo, Viale Antonio Paolucci 5, Venice, Italy;
www.venicebackpackershostel.com/, T:041920711,
info@venicebackpackershostel.com; $27bed>,
Kitchen:N, B'fast:$, WiFi:Y, Pvt. room:Y, Locker:N, Desk hr:24/7;
Note: bar, lounge, parking, a/c, TV, 5 min. walk from train, 4th Fl no lift

Ostello de Venezia, Fondamenta delle Zitelle, 86, 133 Venice, Italy;
www.hostelvenice.org/, T:0415238211, *info@ostellovenezia.it;* $32bed>,
Kitchen:N, B'fast:Y, WiFi:$, Pvt. room:N Locker:Y, Desk hr:24/7;
Note: HI chg, wheelchair ok, resto/bar, c.c. ok, island w/ water taxi, mkt

B&B Best Holidays, Calle delle Beccarie, Pescheria Rialto, San Polo, Italy;
www.bestholidaysvenice.com/, T:+39415242874; $41bed>,
Kitchen:N, B'fast:Y, WiFi:Y, Pvt. room:Y, Locker:N, Desk hr12n>12m;
Note: hard find, cash, check-in next door, advise arrival time, luggage ok

Hotel Astoria, Calle Fiubera, 951, Venice, Italy;
www.hotelastoriavenezia.it, T:0415288981, *info@hotelastoriavenezia.it;* $45bed>,
Kitchen:N, B'fast:$, WiFi:N, Pvt. Room:Y, Locker:N, Desk hr:24/7;
Note: hard to find, good location, luggage room, tour desk, c.c. ok

Youth Venice Home, Sestiere Castello, 3368, Venice, Italy;
http://youthvenicehome.com/, T:3470701833, *youthvenicehome@hotmail.com;*
$39bed>, Kitchen:Y, B'fast:N, WiFi:Y, Pvt. room:Y,
Locker:Y, Desk hr:>12m;
Note: left luggage/linen fee, advise arrival time, bar, free tour, good location

Casa Linger Hostel, 30122 Castello 35/41 Venice, Italy;
www.hotelcasalinger.com/, T:0415285920, *hotelcasalinger@hotmail.com;* $40bed>,
Kitchen:N, B'fast:N, WiFi:N, Pvt. room:Y, Locker:N, Desk hr:>12m;
Note: no Internet, central

A Venice Fish, Sestiere Cannaregio 2205, Campo della Maddalena, Venice;
www.avenicefish.com/ avenicefish@hotmail.com; $34bed>,
Kitchen:N, B'fast:N, WiFi:Y, Pvt. room:N, Locker:N, Desk hr:9a>12m;
Note: age limit 40, bar, linen/towel fee, noon lockout, cash only, laundry

14) Liechtenstein

Liechtenstein is another of those European anomalies, created out of political expedience, in this case for a seat in the Imperial government of the Holy Roman Empire. Its princes didn't set foot here for over a hundred years. Today it is one of the wealthiest countries in the world per capita. At sixty-two square miles (160 square km), Liechtenstein is the sixth smallest independent nation in the world, home to some 35,000 people. It has more companies than people, many of them tax havens (and some specialized laundries ;-). It is a beautiful landlocked country, double-landlocked in fact, i.e. it is surrounded by countries that are themselves landlocked. There is a castle at Vaduz. The town's Fürst Liechtensteinische Gemäldegalerie has some of the art collection of the princes of Liechtenstein. The State Art Collection includes works by 20th century painters, and there's also the Liechtenstein Postal Museum and the Liechtenstein National Museum. The language is German; the currency is the Swiss franc; the calling code is +423.

www.tourismus.li

Y. H. Schaan Vaduz FL, Untere Rüttigasse 6, Schaan, Liechtenstein 9494; *www.youthhostel.ch*, T:+4232325022, *schaan@youthhostel.ch*; $38bed>, Kitchen:N, B'fast:Y, WiFi:Y, Pvt room:N, Locker:Y, Desk hr:5p>9p;
Note: non-HI surcharge, laundry, hard to find, c.c. ok, far, breakfast buffet

15) Luxembourg

Luxembourg is a city and state that grew up around a castle. Strategically, it was home for a succession of Bourbons, Habsburgs and Hohenzollerns, before France and Netherlands and Germany. It finally became a modern state at the same time as Belgium, to which it lost half its territory, all French-speaking, and with which it now forms a trade partnership, along with the Netherlands. Like Belgium and Switzerland, Luxembourg is a north-south border nation that is effectively divided between Romance and Germanic sectors. The standard of living is high. The Old Town is a UNESCO World Heritage site. The major cultural institution of Luxembourg is the Grand Ducal Institute. Then there's The National Museum of History, National Library, the National Archives, and the Music Conservatory of the City of Luxembourg. The currency is Euro, the phone code is +352, and languages are French, German, and Luxembourgish.

www.lcto.lu/en/index

Luxembourg City Hostel, 2 Rue du Fort Olisy, L-2261 Luxembourg; *http://youthhostels.lu/,* T:(+352)22688920, *luxembourg@youthhostels.lu*; $32bed>, Kitchen:N, B'fast:Y, WiFi:Y, Pvt. room:N, Locker:Y, Desk hr:24/7;
Note: resto/bar, parking, terrace, lift, walkable to town

16) Malta

Going to the island of Malta is like time travel, for this tiny country strategically located in the Mediterranean Sea has seen the waves of history wash across its shores for thousands of years, whether Phoenicians, Carthaginians, Greeks, Romans, Normans, Knights Hospitallers, or English. Today Malta is in the Euro-zone, speaks an Arabic dialect, is thoroughly Christian, and claims a cuisine with influences that span the Mediterranean. Sound interesting? The Megalithic Temples here are some of the oldest free-standing structures in the world. The language is Maltese, the currency is the Euro, and the phone country code is +356.

www.visitmalta.com/

SLIEMA may be contiguous to Valletta in a long walk, but is distinctly different. If Valletta is the old historical Malta, Sliema is the new modern one, with many apartment blocks and new hotels. If you want to hang around for a while, this is a good bet.

www.sliema-malta.com/

Hibernia House Gateway Hostel, Depiro St., Sliema, Malta;
www.hihostels.com, T:0035625588000, *emizz@nsts.org;* $40bed>,
Kitchen:Y, B'fast:Y, WiFi:N, Pvt. room:Y, Locker:Y, Desk hr:8a>2p;
Note: café/bar, wheelchairs ok, central, lift, tour desk, c.c. ok, bike rent

VALLETTA is the capital of Malta and a UNESCO world heritage site, with architecture dating from the 16th century. They have a lively Carnival, and the food is good. Sights include the National Museum of Archeology, the National Museum of Fine Arts, the War Museum, the Manoel Theatre, and the National Library of Malta.

www.visitmalta.com/valletta-town

British Hotel, 40 Battery St, Valletta, Malta;
www.britishhotel.com/, T:+35621224730, *info@britishhotel.com;* $34bed>,
Kitchen:N, B'fast:Y, WiFi:Y, Pvt. room:Y, Locker:N, Desk hr:24/7;
Note: private only, bar, restaurant, deck, a/c, c.c. ok, parking, forex

17) Netherlands

In every language the translation is the same, "low lands," and that is the distinguishing feature of the Netherlands, aka "Holland," the fact that much of the country is at or below sea level. The Netherlands were settled early in the Common Era by more or less the same tribes as the ones who settled France, the Franks, southern tribes becoming Romanized while the northern ones maintained their Germanic roots and language, a single linguistic group that forms a continuum across the contiguous German plains. That process of choosing the southern or northern culture still goes on to some extent to this day down south in Belgium. Many of the Jews expelled from Spain in 1492 went to the Netherlands, and the rest is history.

Though tiny, once the Kingdom of the Netherlands freed itself from imperial Spain it went on to establish the next great empire after that of Portugal and Spain, including colonies in South Africa (before the Bantu-speaking Africans themselves got there by the way), Indonesia, South America, and—oh yeah, New Amsterdam, now better known as Nueva York. The English put the kibosh on that little fantasy, of course, but by then Holland was a thoroughly capitalist state, perhaps the first, a step beyond mere free trade and featuring a stock exchange, insurance, retirement funds, boom-bust cycles, asset-inflation, corporate raiders, short sellers, whew!—and well positioned for the future (?!). Today the Netherlands are a bastion of liberal democracy and a founding member of NATO and EU. Dutch is the language, Euro is currency, and phone code is +31.

www.holland.com

AMSTERDAM has much the same history as the Netherlands, of course, as its longtime capital and major city, but these days Netherlands' much-touted liberalism has become stock-in-trade for Amsterdam, in particular its liberal drug laws, which have spawned a cottage industry of cannabis "coffee shops" and related industries. I can't recommend any of this, of course, any more than I can recommend drinking any one of a large number of alcoholic drinks to be found in literally thousands of public houses around the world. This industry threatens to supplant the more traditional sex industry which Amsterdam has long been famous for, in which a red-blooded male can get his rocks off from girls of any one of several dozen different nationalities from all over the world all here for the same reason—to study. They line the windows that line the canals that line the walls of your imagination.

For the less degenerate tourists, there are lovely canals, excellent bike paths, superb museums, and a multitude of entertainment venues. Museums include the Rijksmuseum, the Stedelijk museum, the Van Gogh Museum, and the Anne Frank House. Ancient buildings in the old part of Amsterdam include the Old Church and the New Church, the Royal Palace, the Mint Tower, the South Church, the West Church, the Trippenhuis, and the Old Man's House Gate. Amsterdam has come a long way since its origins as a dam on the River Amstel. It is also well-connected to the rest of Europe, but be forewarned that your Eurolines bus may be searched on arrival in Paris, complete with skunk-sniffing dogs. Amsterdam's motto is *""Leef en laat leven;"* sounds good to me. With Islamic politics and problems from drug tourists, though, there are signs that the famed tolerance is undergoing change. Better hurry. C U at the *Melkveg.*

www.iamsterdam.com/

Hostel Van Gogh, Van de Veldestraat 5, 1071 CW Amsterdam Oud-Zuid; *www.hotelvangogh.nl/*, T:0202629200, *info@hotelvangogh.nl*; $39bed>, Kitchen:Y, B'fast:$, WiFi:Y, Pvt. room:Y, Locker:N, Desk hr:24/7;
Note: dorm age 18-40, a/c, bike hire, laundry, lift, c.c. ok, travel desk

Stayokay Vondelpark, Zandpad 5, 1054 GA Amsterdam Oud-Zuid; *www.stayokay.com/*, T:0205898996, *vondelpark@stayokay.com*; $44bed>, Kitchen:N, B'fast:Y, WiFi:Y, Pvt. room:Y, Locker:Y, Desk hr:24/7;
Note: bar, free tour, travel desk, c.c. ok, lift, big bldg., central, by park

Cocomama, Westeinde 18, 1017 ZP Amsterdam, Netherlands;
www.cocomama.nl/, T:0206272454, *info@cocomama.nl;* $55bed>,
Kitchen:Y, B'fast:N, WiFi:Y, Pvt. room:N, Locker:Y, Desk hr:9a>9p;
Note: check-in 4p, c.c.+2% charge, ex-brothel, "boutique-y", not central

St. Christopher's Inn-Winston, Warmoesstraat 131, 1012 JA Binnenstad;
www.winston.nl/, T:0206231380; $47bed>,
Kitchen:N, B'fast:Y, WiFi:Y, Pvt. room:Y, Locker:Y, Desk hr:24/7;
Note: resto/bar, club, c.c. ok, free tour, travel desk, noisy, red light district

Flying Pig Uptown Hostel, Vossiusstraat 46, 1071 AJ Amsterdam Oud-Zuid;
www.flyingpig.nl/, T:0204004187, *uptown@flyingpig.nl;* $25bed>,
Kitchen:Y, B'fast:Y, WiFi:Y, Pvt. room:N, Locker:Y Desk hr:24/7;
Note: ages 18-40, bar, city tour, c.c. ok, cozy crappers, min. stay 2 nights

Stayokay Stadsdoelen, Kloveniersburgwal 97, 1011 KB Amsterdam;
www.stayokay.com, T:0206246832, *stadsdoelen@stayokay.com;* $35bed>,
Kitchen:N, B'fast:Y, WiFi:Y, Pvt. room:N, Locker:Y, Desk hr:24/7;
Note: laundry, city tour, c.c. ok, central, few sockets

The Bulldog, Oudezijds Voorburgwal 132, 1012 Amsterdam;
www.bulldoghotel.com, T:06270295, *info@bulldoghotel.com;* $46bed>,
Kitchen:N, B'fast:Y, WiFi:Y, Pvt. room:Y, Locker:Y, Desk hr:24/7;
Note: bar, a/c, c.c. ok, city tour, travel desk, laundry, min. stay 2 nights

Hotel Hostel Mevlana, NZ. Voorburgwal 160, 1012 SJ Amsterdam;
www.mevlanahotel.com, T:0203306641, *hotelmevlana@hotmail.com;* $46bed>,
Kitchen:N, B'fast:N, WiFi:Y, Pvt. room:Y, Locker:Y, Desk hr:24/7;
Note: bar, c.c. ok, travel desk, central

Inner Amsterdam, Wanningstraat 1, 1071 LA Amsterdam, Netherlands;
www.innerhotel.nl/, T:0206625792, *info@innerhotel.nl;* $42bed>,
Kitchen:N, B'fast:Y, WiFi:Y, Pvt. room:Y, Locker:N, Desk hr:11p;
Note: c.c. ok, central, BYOB

Hans Brinker Hotel, Kerkstraat 136, 1017 GR Amsterdam, Netherlands;
www.hans-brinker.com/, T:0206220687, *sybil@hans-brinker.com;* $33bed>,

Kitchen:N, B'fast:Y, WiFi:Y, Pvt. room:Y, Locker:Y, Desk hr:24/7;
Note: re-confirm, bar, restaurant, club, left luggage, c.c. ok, central

ROTTERDAM began in 1270 as a dam on the river Rotte, and was until recently the busiest port in the world as well as the sixth most populous conurbation in Europe. A lively competition exists with Amsterdam and The Hague, and, despite Rotterdam's reputation as the workhorse of the group, a lively cultural life exists. Things to see and do include the Boymans-van Beuningen Museum, the Museum of Ethnology, the Prince Henry Maritime Museum, the Historical Museum... and the zoo, of course.

www.rotterdam.nl/

Hostel Room Rotterdam, Van Vollenhovenstraat 62, 3016 BK;
www.roomrotterdam.nl, T:0102827277, *info@roomrotterdam.nl;* $27bed>,
Kitchen:Y, B'fast:Y, WiFi:Y, Pvt. room:N, Locker:Y, Desk hr:24/7;
Note: theme rooms, bar/café, bike rent, free tour, tour desk, c.c. ok

18) Northern Ireland

Not really an independent country properly speaking, Northern Ireland "opted out" of Irish independence and decided to stay with the UK when the rest of Ireland was granted independence in 1921. Ostensibly this was to protect the rights of the Protestant majority in the north, so the upshot was that the minority Catholics were disadvantaged instead. The problem has yet to yield a long-term solution, and is perhaps unsolvable considering that during the "Plantation of Ulster" in the early 1600's, land was confiscated and reserved for Scottish and English colonists who were required to be English-speaking and Protestant, so not much different from Chinese transmigration projects in Tibet today.

The "Troubles" that began on Bloody Sunday 1972 ended home rule for Northern Ireland and lasted until an agreement was finally reached in 1998. The fact that in some areas—Agriculture, Education, Environment, Health, Tourism, and Transport—issues will be handled on an all-island basis, gives hope that old animosities and outdated religious issues will fade in the light of a new era and new modes of cooperation. For the foreseeable future at least, the war is over, and Northern Ireland is wide open for tourism. Currency is the pound, phone code is +44, and languages are English, Irish, and Scots.

www.discovernorthernireland.com/

BELFAST is the major city in Northern Ireland, of course, and an industrial one in the English fashion that it so admires. Shipbuilding is historically one of its specialties, and the *Titanic* was built here. It's a place with a recent history of political "troubles," but that's mostly forgotten these days, and Belfast is open for business, with connections to both the rest of the UK and the Republic of Ireland, too. Still there are neighborhoods segregated between republicans and unionists, so much work yet to do. But it's cheaper over here, so not a bad place to linger, if you have to. Not unlike other secondary markets, hostels here try harder, so high marks for many.

www.belfasttourist.com

Global Village, 87 University St, Belfast, County Antrim UK;
http://globalvillagebelfast.com/, T:+44(0)2890313533; $21bed>, Kitchen:Y, B'fast:Y, WiFi:Y, Pvt. room:Y, Locker:N, Desk hr: 24/7;
Note: towel fee, laundry, bit of a walk

Vagabonds Belfast, 9 University Rd, Belfast, County Antrim UK;
www.vagabondsbelfast.com/, T:02890233017, *info@vagabondsbelfast.com;* $21bed>, Kitchen:Y, B'fast:Y, WiFi:Y, Pvt. room:N, Locker:Y, Desk hr:lmtd;
Note: laundry, lounge

Lagan Backpackers, 121 Fitzroy Ave., Belfast, County Antrim UK;
www.laganbackpackers.com/, T:+44(0)2895140049; $19bed>, Kitchen:Y, B'fast:Y, WiFi:Y, Pvt. room:Y, Locker:N, Desk hr:>11p;
Note: English breakfast, half hour walk to center

Linen House Hostel, 18-20 Kent St, Belfast UK;
www.belfasthostel.com/, T:+44(0)2890586400, *info@belfasthostel.com;* $10bed>, Kitchen:Y, B'fast:N, WiFi:Y, Pvt. room:Y, Locker:N, Desk hr:24/7;
Note: $5 pizza, late night party in basement

Paddy's Palace, 68 Lisburn Road, Belfast, UK;
www.paddyspalace.com/, T:+44(0)2890333367; $18bed>, Kitchen:Y, B'fast:Y, WiFi:Y, Pvt. room:Y, Locker:N, Desk hr:24/7;
Note: Free Giants' Causeway tour

DERRY, aka Londonderry, is Northern Ireland's second city, and best known as the site of resistance to the Unionist government. It dates back to at least the sixth century as a monastic settlement. The old city was walled, the remains of which are one of Europe's finest—and final—examples of such, and Derry's most famous tourist attraction, complete with four gates. That's because it was planned as one of the "Plantations of Ulster" by which British Protestants were "planted" in Ireland to develop it along British lines. It used to be so well-known for shirtmaking that Karl Marx mentioned it in *Das Kapital.* Then there was partition, which put Derry right on the new border-line. The Catholics were unhappy and oppressed. They organized to air their grievances. On January 30, 1972, thirteen unarmed protesters were gunned down by British paratroopers in an event known as Bloody Sunday, which was the start of years of "troubles." It's better now, and Ireland will soon be reunited. You can bank on it, at Lloyd's of London.

www.derryvisitor.com/

Derry City Independent Hostel, 44 Great James St, Londonderry, UK; *www.derryhostel.com,* T:02871280542, *derryhostel@hotmail.com;* $18bed>, Kitchen:Y, B'fast:Y, WiFi:Y, Pvt. room:Y, Locker:N, Desk hr:>10p;
Note: $5 BBQ, pub crawls, free tours, tour desk, parking, c.c. ok

Paddy's Palace, 1 Woodleigh Terrace, Asylum Rd, Londonderry; *www.paddyspalace.com;* T:02871309051; $19bed>, Kitchen:Y, B'fast:Y, WiFi:Y, Pvt. room:Y, Locker:N, Desk hr:lmtd;
Note: free BBQ, parking, TV, tour desk, luggage room, laundry

19) Norway

When you think of countries that border Russia, you don't usually think of Norway, but there it is, sharing the Arctic Ocean with them and Alaska and Canada and Greenland, staking claims to a hypothetical pole and making claims to its hypothetical oil. The historical Norse are probably best remembered for their Vikings, of course, and if the Swedish variety were inward-looking toward the lands now called Russia, and the Danes mostly interested in setting up shop, and "Danelaw,"in the lands now called Britain, the Norwegian branch of the brotherhood were anything but shy in their effort, expanding to the Faroe Islands, Iceland, Greenland, and even America. After various permutations (Norway was absorbed into Denmark for four centuries) and occupation by German Nazis, today Norway, with the help of North Sea oil, is one of the richest countries in the world, and a nice place to hang, too, if you can afford it. Norwegian (Nynorsk or Bokmal) is the language, *krone* is the currency, and the calling code is +47.

www.visitnorway.com/us/

BERGEN is Norway's second city, and its position on the West Coast makes it the capital of the North Sea oil industry in Norway. The Hanseatic-era wharf is a UNESCO world heritage site. Other sites are the 12th C. Saint Mary's Church, the city's oldest structure; Bergenhus fortress; and the Rosenkrantz Tower. Then there's the West Norway Museum of Decorative

Art. The Bergen International Music Festival is an annual event. The Gulf Stream keeps temps mild in winter, but it rains like a mother.

www.planetware.com/map/bergen-map-n-bergen_c.htm

HI Montana Y. H., Johan Blytts vei 30, Bergen, Norway;
www.hihostels.no; T:+4755208070, *bergen.montana@hihostels.no;* $49bed>,
Kitchen:Y, B'fast:Y, WiFi:Y, Pvt. room:Y, Locker:N, Desk hr:>10p;
Note: linen fee $12, wheelchair ok, parking, laundry, c.c. ok, distant

LILLEHAMMER was the site of the 1994 Winter Olympics. The highway from Oslo to Trondheim on the west coast passes through. The city center is of 19th C. wood construction. The open-air Maihaugen folk museum has Norwegian art and architecture.

www.lillehammer.com/en/

Lillehammer Hostel, Jernbanetorget 2, Lillehammer, Norway;
www.815mjosa.no/artikkel/les/160/87/, T:80019572; $52bed>,
Kitchen:Y, B'fast:Y, WiFi:Y, Pvt. room:Y, Locker:N, Desk hr:lmtd;
Note: parking, lift, a/c, c.c. ok, travel desk, located at bus/train station

OSLO is Norway's largest city and capital. Though founded as long ago as 1049, its status as vassal to Denmark reduced its importance and development. Today much of its business is focused around its port and related maritime industries. It is regularly rated as one of the most expensive cities in the world. This is when hostels come in very handy. I'm only surprised that they don't have more of them, possibly because of the low Norwegian population in general. Like its sister cities in the region, Oslo is clean and green, and sixty-degree north latitude means about eighteen hours of daylight in summer and only six in winter. The Gulf Stream keeps the temps moderate, though. There is a Historical Museum and the National Museum of Art, Architecture, and Design. At Tøyen, in the east of the city, are botanical gardens and several museums, including the Munch Museum. At Bygdøy are the Norwegian Folk Museum, the Viking Ship Museum, the Fram Museum, the Kon-Tiki Museum, and the Norwegian shipping museum. Enjoy.

www.visitoslo.com/en/

Perminalen Hotel, Øvre Slottsgate 2, Oslo, Norway; *www.perminalen.no/*, T:24005500, *post.perminalen@iss.no;* $66bed>, Kitchen:N, B'fast:Y, WiFi:Y, Pvt. room:N, Locker:N, Desk hr:24/7; **Note:** luggage room, lift, c.c. ok, clean, central

Oslo Y.H. Haraldsheim, Haraldsheimveien 4, Oslo, Norway; *www.hihostels.no/*, T:22222965, *oslo.haraldsheim@hihostels.no;* $46bed>, Kitchen:Y, B'fast:Y, WiFi:Y, Pvt. room:Y, Locker:Y, Desk hr:24/7; **Note:** linen fee, luggage room, parking, wheelchairs ok, member discount

Sentrum Pensjonat, Tollbugata 8, Oslo, Norway; *www.sentrumpensjonat.no/*, T:22335580, *post@sentrumpensjonat.no*; $50bed>, Kitchen:Y, B'fast:N, WiFi:Y, Pvt. room:Y, Locker:Y, Desk hr:lmtd; **Note:** resto/café, luggage room, forex, c.c. OK, old, central, some residents

Oslo Hotel Apts., Kjølberggaten 29, Oslo, Norway; *www.oslohotelapartments.com/*, T:+4724074003, *booking@kampenhotell.no;* $60bed>, Kitchen:Y, B'fast:$, WiFi:Y, Pvt. room:Y, Locker:N, Desk hr:24/7; **Note:** Resto/bar, parking, luggage ok, linen fee, computer, mixed quality

20) Portugal

Portugal once had an influence far beyond its narrow borders and established the paradigm for the European Age of Discovery, founding colonies on every continent, and at one point collaborating with Spain and the Pope in dividing the world between them. The two countries had similar historical beginnings, but the Portuguese managed to extricate themselves from Moorish oversight more quickly, and was able to proclaim independence in 1139, Europe's first modern nation-state. Somewhere along the way they learned how to sail, and were the first Europeans to sail the open seas, first rounding Africa, and then moving on to Asia and Brazil, in the process establishing the world's first global empire, all from a nation of only a scarce few million people.

Their empire lasted even into the 1970's, though by then Portugal was the poorest country in Western Europe. Its fortunes have improved since shedding itself of its outliers, though still it is no wealthier than you would expect from such a small and largely rural country. So its prices are more like Eastern Europe than the West, and that's good for us tourists. Tourism in fact has exploded in the last decade, major destinations being the sunny southern Algarve coast, the island of Madeira, and the capital Lisbon. Euro is the currency and the telephone country code is +351. Portuguese is the language.

www.visitportugal.com/

COIMBRA is Portugal's third city and a university town. From 1139 to 1260 it was capital of Portugal and base for reconquest from the Moors. The chapel at Universidade de Coimbra has a library with over a million books.

There is also a Romanesque old cathedral, a new cathedral, the church of Sao Salvador, the Machado de Castro Museum, the Santa Cruz church, the Aqueduct of Sao Sebastiao, and the Monastery of Celas. The Rolling Stones played here in 2003 during my visit to Portugal, so I ended up avoiding the place entirely, since there were no rooms available.

www.turismodecoimbra.pt/

Grande Hostel de Coimbra, Rua Antero de Quental 196, Coimbra; *www.grandehostelcoimbra.com,* T:239108212; $20bed>,
Kitchen:Y, B'fast:Y, WiFi:Y, Pvt. room:N, Locker:Y, Desk hr:24/7;
Note: luggage room, laundry, tour desk, c.c. ok, central

Coimbra Youth Hostel, Rua Henrique Seco 14, Coimbra, Portugal; *www.hihostels.com/,* T:+351239822955, *coimbra@movijovem.pt;* $16bed>,
Kitchen:Y, B'fast:Y, WiFi:Y, Pvt. room:Y, Locker:N, Desk hr:24/7;
Note: lockout 12n>6p, central, tour desk, c.c. ok

FARO was the last Moorish stronghold in Portugal and was sacked in 1596 by the Earl of Essex, who pillaged the former bishop's palace library. It was then almost destroyed by the earthquakes of 1722 and 1755. The cathedral was restored and the Convent of Nossa Senhora da Anunciacao is in ruins. Lagos may be ground zero for the Algarve's fun 'n sun, but Faro is the administrative center. This is where your budget airline will land.

http://faro.costasur.com/

Faro Youth Hostel, R. da PSP, Edifício do IPJ, Faro, **Portugal**; *www.hihostels.com,* T:+351289878090, *faro@movijovem.pt;* $17bed>,
Kitchen:Y, B'fast:Y, WiFi:Y, Pvt. room:N, Locker:Y, Desk hr:24/7;
Note: tour desk, c.c. ok, TV, store, forex, discount for members, central

LAGOS was once an historical shipyard and center of the European slave trade, but today it is ground zero for the fun'n sun scene on the Portuguese Algarve, Europe's southernmost strand. Don't forget to wear protection. An SPF rating of at least 15 is usually recommended.

www.lagos.me.uk/

Stumble Inn, Rua Soeiro da Costa 10, Lagos, Portugal; *www.stumbleinnlagos.com/*, T:282607081, *stumbleinnlagos@gmail.com;* $26bed>, Kitchen:Y, B'fast:N, WiFi:Y, Pvt. room:Y, Locker:N, Desk hr:24/7; **Note:** bar, forex, free tour, parties, bar next door, central

Lagos Escape Hostel, Rua Gil Vicente 26, Lagos, Portugal; *www.lagos-escape-hostel.com/*, T:915198414, *info@lagos-escape-hostel.com;* $20bed>, Kitchen:N, B'fast:Y, WiFi:Y, Pvt. room:N, Locker:Y, Desk hr:24/7; **Note:** bar, laundry, c.c. ok, safe, terrace, central, parties

Casa Sousa, Rua do Jogo da Bola nº 17, Lagos, Portugal; *www.casa-sousa.com/*, T:282089461, *casa.sousa@hotmail.com;* $24bed>, Kitchen:Y, B'fast:N, WiFi:Y, Pvt. room:Y, Locker:N, Desk hr:24/7; **Note:** cash only, 2N min. stay, central, close to beach

Rising Cock Hostel, Travessa do Forno 14, Lagos, Portugal; *www.risingcock.com/*, T:968758785, *info@risingcock.com;* $39bed>, Kitchen:Y, B'fast:Y, WiFi:Y, Pvt. room:N, Locker:Y, Desk hr:24/7; **Note:** party, Mama's crepes, party, booze cruise, restaurant, party anyone?

Cloud 9 Hostel, Rua Soeiro da Costa 9, 8600-624 Lagos, Portugal; *www.cloud9hostel.com/*, T:282183355, *cloud9hostel@gmail.com;* $20bed>, Kitchen:Y, B'fast:N, WiFi:N, Pvt. room:Y, Locker:Y, Desk hr:24/7; **Note:** bar, laundry, city tour, bike hire, central

LISBON (Lisboa) is the capital and largest city of Portugal and shares its history from the beginning. As such it was one of the most important cities in the world in the 16th century. Unfortunately it was also earthquake-prone and had many. The worst was in 1755, which resulted in a tsunami that killed some ten percent of the population and devastated coastal areas from Britain to Morocco. The city was rebuilt in a more modern style, much of which remains today. Today the city has much entertainment and many festivals, especially in summer. And for those of us who like our nostalgia in dimly-lit clubs, listening to some *fado* in the old Alfama district can be quite worthwhile. Portuguese bullfighting can be witnessed at the old red-brick *Campo Pequeno*. The Tower of Belem, located on the riverbank, is a UN World Heritage site. No place exemplifies the current European hostel explosion better than Lisbon. Quality is very high. Many of these places qualify as "best ever" for many travelers.

www.visitlisboa.com/

Traveller's House, R. Augusta 89, Lisbon, Portugal;
www.travellershouse.com/, T:210115922, *info@travellershouse.com;* $28bed>,
Kitchen:Y, B'fast:Y, WiFi:Y, Pvt. room:N, Locker:Y, Desk hr:24/7;
Note: coffee/tea, c.c. ok, laundry, books, TV, activities, happy hour, wine

Lisboa Central Hostel, R. Rodrigues Sampaio 160, Lisbon, Portugal;
www.lisboacentralhostel.com, T: 309881038, *global@lisboacentralhostel.com;*
$27bed>, Kitchen:Y, B'fast:Y, WiFi:Y, Pvt. room:Y, Locker:Y, Desk hr:24/7;
Note: luggage ok, coffee & tea, bar, laundry, games, activities, pancakes!

This is Lisbon Hostel, Rua da Costa do Castelo 63, Lisbon;
www.thisislisbonhostel.com/, T:218014549, *info@thisislisbonhostel.com;* $21bed>,
Kitchen:Y, B'fast:Y, WiFi:Y, Pvt. room:Y, Locker:Y, Desk hr:24/7;
Note: coffee & tea, good location, great views, laundry, bar, tour desk

Living Lounge Hostel, Rua do Crucifixo 116, Lisbon, Portugal;
www.lisbonloungehostel.com/, T:213461078, *info@livingloungehostel.com;*
$28bed>, Kitchen:Y, B'fast:Y, WiFi:Y, Pvt. room:N, Locker:Y, Desk hr:24/7;
Note: bar, laundry, tour desk, meals, stairs, left luggage, free tour

Lisbon Poets' Hostel, Rua Nova da Trindade 2, Lisbon, Portugal;
www.lisbonpoetshostel.com/, T:213461241, *lisbonpoetshostel@gmail.com;* $26bed>,
Kitchen:Y, B'fast:Y, WiFi:Y, Pvt. room:Y, Locker:Y, Desk hr:24/7;
Note: c.c. ok, min. stay 4N, good location, tour desk, laundry

Alfama Patio Hostel, Escolas Gerais 3, Lisbon, Portugal;
http://alfamapatio.com/, T:218883127, *contact@alfamapatio.com;* $24bed>,
Kitchen:Y, B'fast:Y, WiFi:Y, Pvt. room:Y, Locker:Y, Desk hr:24/7;
Note: bar, free tour, laundry, tour desk, c.c. ok, activities, non-touristy

Lisbon Chillout Hostel, Rua Nogueira e Sousa, Lisbon, Portugal;
www.lisbonchillouthostel.com/, T:212468450, *lisbonchh@gmail.com;* $20bed>,

Kitchen:Y, B'fast:Y, WiFi:Y, Pvt. room:Y, Locker:Y, Desk hr:24/7;
Note: bar, lounge, c.c. ok. Laundry, activities, coffee & tea

Equity Point Lisboa, Travessa do Fala-Só 9, Lisbon, Portugal;
www.equity-point.com/, T:218018211, *infolisboa@equity-point.com;* $20bed>,
Kitchen:Y, B'fast:Y, WiFi:Y, Pvt. room:Y, Locker:Y, Desk hr:24/7;
Note: bar, tour desk, c.c. ok, top of a hill, central, not a party hostel

Lisbon Lounge Hostel, R. de São Nicolau 41, Lisbon, Portugal;
www.lisbonloungehostel.com/, T:213462061, *info@lisbonloungehostel.com;*
$26bed>, Kitchen:Y, B'fast:Y, WiFi:Y, Pvt. room:N, Locker:Y, Desk hr:24/7;
Note: bar, restaurant, laundry, tour desk, quiet area, eggs

Lisbon Old Town Hostel, R. do Ataíde 26A, Lisbon, Portugal;
*www.lisbonoldtownhostel.com,*_T: 213465248, *lisbonoldtownhostel@gmail.com;*
$22bed>, Kitchen:Y, B'fast:Y, WiFi:Y, Pvt. room:N, Locker:Y, Desk hr:24/7;
Note: c.c. ok, wheelchair ok, laundry, spacious

People Hostel, R. dos Jerónimos 16, Lisboa, Portugal;
www.peoplehostel.com/, T:218289567, *geral@peoplehostel.com;* $13bed>,
Kitchen:Y, B'fast:Y, WiFi:Y, Pvt. room:Y, Locker:N, Desk hr:24/7;
Note: left luggage, laundry, bar, laundry, c.c. ok, clean cute cozy

Go Hostel Lisbon, Rua Maria da Fonte 55, Lisbon, Portugal;
www.gohostellisbon.com/, T:218229816, *gohostellisbon@gmail.com;* $16bed>,
Kitchen:Y, B'fast:Y, WiFi:Y, Pvt. room:Y, Locker:Y, Desk hr:24/7;
Note: bar, games, free tour, laundry, c.c. ok, garden, mansion, dodgy area

Smile Hostel, Travesa do Almada N° 12 3DRT, Lisbon;
www.smilehostel.com/, T:963736683, *smilehostel@hotmail.com;* $24bed>,
Kitchen:Y, B'fast:Y, WiFi:Y, Pvt. room:Y, Locker:Y, Desk hr:24/7;
Note: a/c, c.c. ok, tour desk, no sign, stairs, central, good brek, min. 2N

Oasis Backpackers' Mansion, R. de Santa Catarina 24, Lisbon;
http://hostelsoasis.com/, T:213478044, *lisboa@hostelsoasis.com;* $13bed>,
Kitchen:Y, B'fast:Y, WiFi:Y, Pvt. room:Y, Locker:Y, Desk hr:24/7;
Note: bar, fado & surf tours, luggage ok, welcome drink, c.c. ok

Lisbon Shiado Hostel, Rua Anchieta 5, Lisbon, Portugal; *www.shiadohostel.com/*, T:213429227, *shiado.hostel@gmail.com;* $22bed>, Kitchen:Y, B'fast:Y, WiFi:Y, Pvt. room:Y, Locker:Y, Desk hr:24/7;
Note: c.c. over $250 ok, left luggage, a/c, city tour, TV, central

Royal Lisbon Hostel, Praça Luís de Camões nr 22-3° Dt, Lisbon; *www.royallisbon.com/*, T:218006797, *info@royallisbon.com*; $24bed>, Kitchen:Y, B'fast:Y, WiFi:Y, Pvt. room:Y, Locker:Y, Desk hr:24/7;
Note: bar, laundry, c.c. ok, good location, noisy at night

Unreal Hostel Lisboa, Rua Pedro Nunes 10, Lisbon, Portugal; *www.wix.com/unrealhostel*, T:213153101, *info@unrealhostel.com*; $22bed>, Kitchen:N, B'fast:Y, WiFi:Y, Pvt. room:Y, Locker:Y, Desk hr:24/7;
Note: residential neighborhood, few outlets, free laundry

Next Hostel, Avenida Almirante Reis 4, Lisbon, Portugal; *www.nexthostel.com/*, T:211927746; $14bed>, Kitchen:N, B'fast:Y, WiFi:Y, Pvt. room:Y, Locker:Y, Desk hr:24/7;
Note: c.c. ok, central

Residencia Nazareth, Ave. António Augusto de Aguiar 25, 1000 Lisbon; *www.residencianazareth.com/*, T:213542016, *info@residencianazareth.com;* $24bed>, Kitchen:N, B'fast:Y, WiFi:$, Pvt. room:Y, Locker:N, Desk hr:24/7;
Note: a/c, c.c. ok, bar, safe, central, convenient to airport

Jardim de Santos, Largo Vitorino Damásio 4, 1200-872 Lisbon; *www.jardimdesantoshostel.com;*T:213974666; $25bed>, Kitchen:N, B'fast:Y, WiFi:N, Pvt. room:N, Locker:Y, Desk hr:24/7;
Note: luggage room, laundry, c.c. ok

PORTO (Oporto) is Portugal's second city, far to the north on the Atlantic coast, and its old name *Portus Cale* gives Portugal **its** name. This is where Prince Henry the navigator initiated his exploration of the world. Its entire traditional center is a UNESCO world heritage site. Its major export is port wine (burp), *yeah.* The Maria Pia Bridge was designed by Gustave Eiffel. Notable buildings are Porto's cathedral, built on the Visigothic citadel, the church of Sao Martinho de Cedofeita, the Torre dos Clerigos, the Basilica of Sao Francisco, and the stock exchange. This would be a good stopover on a trip between Lisbon and the Basque country. As with all of Portugal, many of the hostels are new and the quality is very high.

www.visitporto.travel/

Porto Spot Hostel, Rua de Gonçalo Cristóvão 12, Oporto; *www.spothostel.pt/,* T:224085205, *bookings@spothostel.pt;* $24bed>, Kitchen:Y, B'fast:Y, WiFi:Y, Pvt. room:Y, Locker:Y, Desk hr:24/7; **Note:** bar, laundry, city tour, activities

Rivoli Cinema Hostel, R. Dr. Magalhães Lemos 83, Oporto, Portugal; *www.rivolicinemahostel.com/,* T:220174634, *rivolicinemahostel@gmail.com;* $26bed>, Kitchen:Y, B'fast:Y, WiFi:Y, Pvt. room:Y, Locker:Y, Desk hr:24/7; **Note:** bar, laundry, tour desk, rooftop terrace, parties, hard to find

Oporto Poets Hostel, Rua dos Caldeireiros 261, Oporto, Portugal; *www.oportopoetshostel.com/,* T:223324209, *oportopoetshostel@gmail.com;* $29bed>, Kitchen:Y, B'fast:Y, WiFi:Y, Pvt. room:N, Locker:Y, Desk hr:24/7; **Note:** c.c. ok, laundry, parking, city tour, dinners, activities

Oporto Sky Hostel, Rua da Lapa 33, Oporto, Portugal; *www.oportosky.com* T:222017069, *info@oportosky.com;* $20bed>, Kitchen:Y, B'fast:Y, WiFi:Y, Pvt. room:Y, Locker:Y, Desk hr:24/7; **Note:** bar, café, market, laundry, tour desk, activities, central

Steps House, Escadas do Monte dos Judeus 5, Oporto, Portugal; *www.stepshouse.hostel.com/,* T:224054051; $20bed>, Kitchen:Y, B'fast:Y, WiFi:Y, Pvt. room:Y, Locker:Y, Desk hr:lmtd; **Note:** c.c. ok, tour desk, bike hire, left luggage, hard to find, lots of steps

Yellow House, Rua de João das Regras 96, Oporto, Portugal; *www.yellowhouse.hostel.com/,* T:222014229; $18bed>, Kitchen:Y, B'fast:Y, WiFi:Y, Pvt. room:N, Locker:Y, Desk hr:lmtd; **Note:** left luggage, c.c. ok, parking, can be cold, bike hire

Porto Riad Guesthouse, Rua D. Joao IV 990, Porto, Portugal; *www.portoriad.com/,* T:225107643, *info@portoriad.com;* $25bed>,

Kitchen:Y, B'fast:Y, WiFi:Y, Pvt. room:Y, Locker:N, Desk hr:24/7;
Note: Moroccan theme, hard to find, a/c, laundry, c.c. ok, wheelchair ok

Tattva Design Hostel, Rua do Cativo 26-28, Porto, Portugal;
http://tattvadesignhostel.com/, T:220944622, *tattvadesignhostel@gmail.com;*
$20bed>, Kitchen:Y, B'fast:Y, WiFi:N, Pvt. room:Y, Locker:Y, Desk hr:24/7;
Note: a/c, c.c. ok, laundry, bar, restaurant, lift, modern, handicap OK

Garden House Hostel, R. de Santa Catarina 501 Porto, Portugal;
http://gardenhousehostelporto.com, T:222081426, *gardenhouse501@gmail.com;*
$20bed>, Kitchen:Y, B'fast:Y, WiFi:Y, Pvt. room:Y, Locker:Y, Desk hr:24/7;
Note: left luggage, a/c, c.c. ok, bar, laundry, city tour, big rooms

Porto Downtown Hostel, Praça de Guilherme Fernandes 66 Oporto;
www.portodowntownhostel.com/, T:222018094; $22bed>,
Kitchen:Y, B'fast:Y, WiFi:Y, Pvt. room:N, Locker:Y, Desk hr:24/7;
Note: ATM, café, laundry, tour desk, central

21) San Marino

Originally established as a refuge from Diocletian's persecution of Christians in 301, today San Marino is the world's smallest republic with only 30,000 people. It is totally surrounded by Italy in its remote mountain three-peak stronghold. It has the world's oldest constitution. Access is from the Italian city of Rimini. Italian is the language; Euro is the currency; calling code is +378.

www.sanmarinosite.com

Hostel San Marino, Via 28 Luglio, 224, Borgo Maggiore, San Marino; *www.hostel-sanmarino.com/*, T:0549922515, *info@hostel-sanmarino.com;* $26bed>, Kitchen:N, B'fast:$, WiFi:Y, Pvt. room:Y, Locker:Y, Desk hr:lmtd; **Note:** bar, parking a/c, c.c. ok, linen fee, free coffee, far from center

22) Scotland

Scotland occupies the northern third of the island of Great Britain in addition to some 790 islands that come with the territory. The Picts, an earlier Celtic Brythonic-speaking group presumably related to the Welsh, were there first. Gaels emigrated from Ireland to form the western province of Dal Riata mid-first-millennium to eventually form a united Pictish Kingdom that was increasingly Gaelic. After the Norman conquest of England in 1066, though, English speakers steadily filtered into the lowlands, relegating the Gaelic cultures to the highlands. An era of peace and stability ended in 1296 with the Scottish wars of independence (from England) and an alliance with France that included participation in the 100 Years War against England. England and Protestantism ultimately prevailed and after a famine that killed twenty percent of its populace, Scotland entered into an act of union with England in 1707. Great prosperity followed for Scotland as a full member of the British Empire and Industrial Revolution.

The Scottish Enlightenment that followed was second to none and gave Scotland a great reputation for its ideas, its science, and its arts. They were not peripheral to Britain's success around the world; there were instrumental to it, and much the same holds true for the two countries today. If they hit a rough patch for a while there, it's mostly forgotten as Scotland's fortunes grow along with North Sea oil, and a partial return to self-government has quelled calls for complete secession. "Scottishness" has lost little over the years. The widely-spoken Scots dialect is a form of old English that developed independently of the English standard in the days of French rule there, becoming mutually unintelligible at some point. Gaelic speakers are few and far between, gradually diminishing until relegated to highland enclaves and the far west coast. The phone code is +44. The currency is the pound. Scottish pounds may be hard to pass in England; vice versa is no problem. And no, the Firth of Forth is not a fraction.

www.visitscotland.com/

ABERDEEN is Scotland's third largest city after Glasgow and Edinburgh. It is the center of the North Sea oil industry, which has largely replaced the traditional fishing and paper-making industries. The climate is mild for such a northern latitude. Ironically some of the oldest landmarks survive in New Aberdeen, near the Castlegate, which still contains an old Market (City) Cross and two ancient houses, Provost Skene's House and Provost Ross's House. Others are the Music Hall and Marischal College on Broad Street.

www.aberdeen-grampian.com/

Aberdeen SYHA Hostel, 8 Queen's Road, Aberdeen, Scotland, UK;
www.syha.org.uk/, T:01224646988, *Aberdeen@syha.org.uk*; $32bed>,
Kitchen:Y, B'fast:N, WiFi:Y, Pvt. room:Y, Locker:N, Desk hr:7a>2a;
Note: luggage room, laundry, parking, c.c. ok

EDINBURGH is the historic heart of Scotland, intellectually, economically and culturally. It is also the capital and second-largest city. This was one of Europe's prime centers of the Enlightenment a few centuries ago and one of the UK's prime tourist attractions now. The Old Town and New Town are both UNESCO World Heritage sites. The Edinburgh Festival held through the entire month of August is a collection of individual festivals that includes the top-rated Fringe festival. The castle is the city's top tourist draw. The old town contains the cathedral of St. Giles, the Parliament House, the City Chambers, and the Market Cross, hub of the old city. The new town, approved in 1767, was intended for people "of a certain rank and fortune." Yeah, right, sounds boring. The railway changed all that. Hostel quality and locations are generally good.

www.edinburgh-inspiringcapital.com/

Castle Rock Hostel, 15 Johnston Terrace, Edinburgh, Scotland, UK;
*http://castlerockedinburgh.com/,*T:01312259666,
castlerock@macbackpackerstours.com; $22bed>,
Kitchen:Y, B'fast:$, WiFi:N, Pvt. room:Y, Locker:Y, Desk hr:24/7;
Note: by Castle, free coffee, theme rooms, few sockets, live-in students

Caledonian Backpackers, 3 Queensferry St, Edinburgh, Scotland UK;
http://caledonianbackpackers.com/, T:+44(0)1314767224; $20bed>,
Kitchen:Y, B'fast:Y, WiFi:Y, Pvt. room:N, Locker:Y, Desk hr:24/7;
Note: bar, free city tour, c.c. ok, laundry, brekkie 7-12, noise at night

Budget Backpackers, 39 Cowgate, Grassmarket, Edinburgh, Scotland UK;
www.budgetbackpackers.com/, T:01312266351, hi@budgetbackpackers.com;
$22bed>, Kitchen:Y, B'fast:N, WiFi:N, Pvt. room:Y, Locker:Y, Desk hr:24/7;
Note: bar/café, free city tour, pub crawls, party hostel

St. Cristopher's Inn Market St., Edinburgh, Midlothian, Scotland UK;
www.st-christophers.co.uk/, T:01312261446, *feedback@st-christophers.co.uk;*
$31bed>, Kitchen:N, B'fast:Y, WiFi:Y, Pvt. room:N, Locker:N, Desk hr:24/7;
Note: min. stay 2N, central, close to train, bar

Royal Mile Backpackers, 105 High St, Edingurgh, Scotland UK;
www.royalmilebackpackers.com/, T:01315576120,
royalmile@scotlandstophostels.com; $21bed>,
Kitchen:Y, B'fast:$, WiFi:Y, Pvt. room:N, Locker:Y, Desk hr:lmtd;
Note: free coffee & tea, long-term rates available

Westend Hotel, 35 Palmerston Place, Edinburgh, Midlothian UK;
www.thewestendhotel.co.uk/, T:01312253656, *info@thewestendhotel.co.uk;*
$20bed>, Kitchen:Y, B'fast:$, WiFi:Y, Pvt. room:N, Locker:N, Desk hr:>11p;
Note: few power outlets, bar, historic building

Argyle Backpackers, 14 Argyle Place, Edinburgh, Midlothian UK;
www.argyle-backpackers.co.uk/, T:01316679991,
reception@argyle-backpackers.co.uk; $21bed>,
Kitchen:Y, B'fast:$, WiFi:Y, Pvt. room:Y, Locker:Y, Desk hr:9a>10p;
Note: free coffee/tea, c.c. ok, laundry, tour desk

High St. Hostel, 8 Blackfriars St, Old Town, Edinburgh, Scotland UK; *http://highstreethostel.com/*, T:+441315573984; $21bed>,
Kitchen:Y, B'fast:$, WiFi:Y, Pvt. room:N, Locker:Y, Desk hr:24/7;
Note: stairs, few power outlets, cozy rooms

Edinburgh Central Hostel, 9 Haddington Pl, Edinburgh, Scotland UK; *www.syha.org.uk/,* T:+44(0)8701553255, *reservations@syha.org.uk*; $37bed>,
Kitchen:Y, B'fast:$, WiFi:Y, Pvt. room:Y, Locker:Y, Desk hr:24/7;
Note: laundry, bar, tour desk, good location

Brodies 93 Hostel, Royal Mile 93 High St, Edinburgh, Scotland UK; www.brodieshostels.co.uk, T:01315562223, *bookings@brodieshostels.co.uk;* $25bed>, Kitchen:Y, B'fast:N, WiFi:$, Pvt. room:N, Locker:$, Desk hr:lmtd;
Note: free coffee & tea, laundry, hard to find, good view

GLASGOW is Scotland's largest city and the UK's third. If Edinburgh is the cultural and intellectual heart of Scotland, Glasgow is the industrial heart. It came to prominence with the Industrial Revolution and the British Empire for its shipbuilding and engineering. Prior to that, it was a trading city with an annual fair. The tobacco trade was very important at one time. The slums were reportedly horrific. Today it is being reinvented as a green city with culture, with many previously rundown areas gone upscale to lure back the upper classes that fled to the suburbs. Merchant City is now a "culture quarter." Ancient buildings are few, just the cathedral and the oldest house of Provand's Lordship, but the historic district of Glasgow Cross has buildings from the 17th and 18th centuries. Museums include Kelvingrove Art Gallery and Museum, The Burrell Collection, the Gallery of Modern Art and the Lighthouse. Then there's the Glasgow Science Center. West End is the bohemian district. The music scene is lively.

www.seeglasgow.com/

Glasgow Youth Hostel, 8 Park Terrace, Glasgow, Lanarkshire UK; *www.syha.org.uk/,* T:+44(0)1413323004; $29bed>,
Kitchen:Y, B'fast:$, WiFi:$, Pvt. room:N, Locker:Y, Desk hr: 24/7;
Note: nice Victorian house, hard to find, stairs, SYHA quality

Queen's Park Budget Hotel, 10 Balvicar Dr., Glasgow, Scotland UK; *www.budgethotelsglasgow.co.uk/*, T:01414231123, *info@budgethotelsglasgow.co.uk;* $17bed>, Kitchen:Y, B'fast:Y, WiFi:Y, Pvt. room:Y, Locker:N, Desk hr:24/7;
Note: c.c. ok, in-room breakfast, far from center

Bunkum Hostel, 26 Hillhead St., Glasgow, Lanarkshire UK; *www.bunkumglasgow.co.uk*, T:01415814481, *BunkumGlasgow@hotmail.com;* $25bed>, Kitchen:Y, B'fast:N, WiFi:Y, Pvt. oom:N, Locker:Y, Desk hr:>10p;
Note: university area, bit of a hike, stairs, free tea/coffee, good name

Alba Hostel, 6 Fifth Ave, Anniesland, Glasgow, Scotland UK; *www.albalodge.co.uk/*, T:01413322588, *info@ albalodge.co.uk;* $24bed>, Kitchen:Y, B'fast:$, WiFi:Y, Pvt. room:N, Locker:Y, Desk hr:24/7;
Note: no locks on doors, long way to center

Bluesky Hostel, 65 Berkeley St, Glasgow, Scotland UK; *www.blueskyhostel.com/* T:01412211710, *blueskyhostel@btconnect.com;* $20bed>, Kitchen:Y, B'fast:N, WiFi:Y, Pvt. room:Y, Locker:Y, Desk hr:8a>12m;
Note: age 18-35, free tea/coffee, WiFi in room, few sockets, central, dog

FORT WILLIAM is the largest town in the Scottish Highlands, second only to the city of Inverness. It is also a major tourist center, due to its proximity to Ben Nevis (that's a peak), the highest point in the UK at 4409ft/1344m (no snickering). With Fort William at sea level, though, along the Great Glen strike/slip fault that dissects northernmost Scotland, 4409 feet is plenty. There are still Gaelic speakers here. "Rob Roy," "Highlander" and "Braveheart" were filmed here.

http://visit-fortwilliam.co.uk/

Fort William Backpackers, Alma Rd, Fort William, Scotland UK; *http://fortwilliambackpackers.com*, T:+44(0)1397700711; $24bed>, Kitchen:Y, B'fast:$, WiFi:Y, Pvt. room:N, Locker:N, Desk hr:8a>10p;
Note: noon lockout, tour desk, parking, c.c. ok, living room/fireplace

Bank Street Lodge, Bank St, Fort William, Scotland UK; *www.bankstreetlodge.co.uk/*, T:01397700070, *bankstreetlodge@btconnect.com;*

$26bed>, Kitchen:Y, B'fast:N, WiFi:Y, Pvt. room:Y, Locker:N, Desk hr:24/7; Note: restaurant, parking, laundry, c.c. ok, near train, cozy rooms, central

Glen Nevis SYHA, Glen Nevis, Fort William, Scotland UK; *www.hihostels.com/,* T:+441397702336, *glen.nevis@syha.org.uk;* $32bed>, Kitchen:Y, B'fast:N, WiFi:$, Pvt. room:Y, Locker:N, Desk hr:7a>11p; **Note:** restaurant, parking, laundry, c.c. ok, not central, few buses

Farr Cottage Lodge, Farr Cottage, Corpach, Fort William, UK; *www.farrcottage.com*, T:01397772315, *mail@farrcottage.com*; $24bed>, Kitchen:Y, B'fast:$, WiFi:Y, Pvt. room:Y, Locker:N, Desk hr:>10p; Note: check-in 1630, bar, prkng, luggage ok, laundry, c.c. ok, bus>center

Chase the Wild Goose Hostel, Banavie by Fort William UK; *www.great-glen-hostel.com;* T:01397748044, *enquiries@great-glen-hostel.com;* $25bed>, Kitchen:Y, B'fast:$, WiFi:$, Pvt. room:N, Locker:N, Desk hr:>11p; **Note:** TV, parking, laundry, luggage room

INVERNESS is the unofficial capital of the Scottish Highlands. It's also one of Europe's fastest-growing cities. Now you're getting into some true north country, up around fifty-five degrees north latitude, farther north than Moscow or Copenhagen. In the summer, you can get transportation even farther north, to the Orkney Islands or the Shetlands, if you're truly motivated. For most travelers, though, it's the jumping-off point to Loch Ness; InverNESS, get it? It's a former Pict stronghold. It's a university town. There are music festivals. It's a center of Scots traditional culture. It's beautiful country; beware of monsters. Hostel quality is good. And, oh yeah, there's a castle.

www.explore-inverness.com/

Bazpackers Hostel, 4 Culduthel Rd, Inverness, Scotland UK; *www.bazpackershostel.co.uk/*; T:+44(0)1463717663; $23bed>, Kitchen:Y, B'fast:N, WiFi:Y, Pvt. room:Y, Locker:Y, Desk hr:8a>11p; **Note:** close to castle, free coffee and tea, laundry, c.c. ok

Inverness Student Hostel, 8 Culduthel Rd, Inverness, Scotland UK; *http://invernessstudenthotel.com/*, T:+44(0)1463236556; $24bed>,

Kitchen:Y, B'fast:$, WiFi:$, Pvt. room:N, Locker:N, Desk hr:lmtd;
Note: free coffee and tea, c.c. ok, laundry, parking, tour desk

Inverness Tourist Hostel, 24 Rose St, Inverness, Scotland UK;
www.invernesshostel.com/, T:01463241962, *info@invernesshostel.com;* $18bed>,
Kitchen:Y, B'fast:N, WiFi:Y, Pvt. room:Y, Locker:Y, Desk hr:>11p;
Note: free coffee and tea, loud club next door, convenient to all

Inverness Milburn Hostel, Victoria Drive, Inverness, Scotland UK;
www.syha.org.uk/, T:01463231771; $30bed>,
Kitchen:Y, B'fast:$, WiFi:$, Pvt. room:Y, Locker:N, Desk hr:lmtd;
Note: bit far, midday lockout, member SYHA, c.c. ok

Eastgate Backpackers Hostel, 38 Eastgate, Inverness, Scotland UK;
www.eastgatebackpackers.com/, T:+44(0)1463718756; $23bed>,
Kitchen:Y, B'fast:N, WiFi:N, Pvt. room:Y, Locker:Y, Desk hr:lmtd;
Note: stairs, midday lockout

ISLE OF SKYE is the largest and most northern of the Inner Hebrides, though you might not even know it's an island if you haven't been there or looked at the map carefully. It's even connected to the mainland by bridge now. More importantly, this is one of the last bastions of Gaelic language and culture. Portree, the largest town, has less than 2000 people. There are Mesolothic and Neolothic remains, but little evidence of the long Norse and Viking presence of the Middle Ages. The Highland Clearances of the mainland occurred here, too, and tenant farmers were dispossessed of their land to allow wealthy landowners to raise sheep. Things are calmer now; tourism is healthy, and the island is experiencing a renewal. There is a lively music and arts scene. Single malt whiskey is made here.

www.skye.co.uk/

Skye Backpackers, Kyleakin, Isle of Skye, Scotland UK;
http://skyebackpackers.com, T:+44(0)1599534510; $19bed>,
Kitchen:Y, B'fast:$, WiFi:Y, Pvt. room:N, Locker:N, Desk hr:8a>10p;
Note: checkin 5pm, noon lockout, parking, c.c. ok, day tours, tea/coffee

Isle of Skye - Broadford SYHA, Broadford, Isle of Skye, **Scotland** UK;
www.hihostels.com/, T:01471822442, *broadford@syha.org.uk;* $28bed>,
Kitchen:Y, B'fast:N, WiFi:Y, Pvt. room:Y, Locker:N, Desk hr:8a>10p;
Note: store, garden, laundry, c.c. ok, parking

Broadford Backpackers Hostel, Broadford, Isle of Skye, **Scotland** UK;
www.broadfordbackpackers.co.uk, T:01471820333,
broadfordbackpackers@gmail.com $30bed>,
Kitchen:Y, B'fast:N, WiFi:Y, Pvt. room:Y, Locker:N, Desk hr:9a>11p;
Note: wheelchair ok, luggage room, laundry, parking, c.c. ok

Saucy Mary's Lodge, Main St, Kyleakin, Isle of Skye, **Scotland** UK;
www.saucymarys.com/, T:01599534845, *saucymarys1@btconnect.com;* $23bed>,
Kitchen:Y, B'fast:$, WiFi:Y, Pvt. room:Y, Locker:N, Desk hr:lmtd;
Note: resto/bar, wheelchair ok, parking, tour desk, c.c. ok, sea view

LOCH NESS is a large lake in Northern Scotland and home to the cryptozoological (I like that word) Loch Ness monster, whose existence is about as likely as the aliens that have visited this planet repeatedly over the millennia. It lies along the Great Glen Fault and with its great depth is the largest lake by volume in the UK.

www.lochnesswelcome.co.uk/

Moarag's Lodge, Fort Augustus, Loch Ness, Scotland UK;
www.moragslodge.com/, T:01320366289, *info@moragslodge.com;* $32bed>,
Kitchen:Y, B'fast:$, WiFi:Y, Pvt. room:Y, Locker:Y, Desk hr:lmtd;
Note: bar w/fire & live music, meals, parking, laundry, c.c. ok, tea/coffee

Loch Ness Hostel, Glenmoriston, Loch Ness, Scotland UK;
www.syha.org.uk/, T:01320351274, *lochness@syha.org.uk;* $32bed>,
Kitchen:Y, B'fast:$, WiFi:Y, Pvt. room:Y, Locker:N, Desk hr:5p>10p;
Note: laundry, parking, c.c. ok

OBAN is a picturesque west coast seaside town of some 8000 people that can swell to over 25,000 at the height of the tourist season. It occupies a beautiful location on a bay in the Firth of Lom. It grew up around a distillery.

www.oban.org.uk/

Oban Backpackers, Breadalbane St, Oban, Scotland UK; *www.obanbackpackers.com/*, T:1631567189, *info@backpackersplus.com*; $34bed>, Kitchen:Y, B'fast:Y, WiFi:Y, Pvt. room:N, Locker:N, Desk hr:lmtd; **Note:** luggage room, laundry, tour desk, c.c. ok

Oban Hostel, Esplanade, Oban, Scotland UK; *www.syha.org.uk/*, T:01631562025, *oban@syha.org.uk*; $32bed>, Kitchen:Y, B'fast:$, WiFi:Y, Pvt. room:Y, Locker:N, Desk hr:24/7; Note: laundry, parking, c.c. ok, good views

23) Spain

Last bastion of Neanderthals and place of high culture for Cro-Magnons, Spain entered the historical age populated by Celts, Iberians, and Basques. Phoenicians and Greeks founded trading colonies, until the Romans finally conquered and assimilated it totally, calling it Hispania. All Hell broke loose in the 5th century AD with the weakening and eventual fall of Rome, of course, but the country was reunited under the Visigoths. Muslim Moors arrived in 711 to conquer the country and ruled an ever-diminshing colony there until 1492, the same year that Columbus's discovery of America heralded Spain's arrival on the world stage with the Age of Discovery. That lasted over three hundred years before a decline set in that saw Spain lose almost all of its overseas colonies and then the establishment of a fascist government under Francisco Franco from 1939-1975. With Franco's death, Spain rejoined the European community of which it is now a full member.

For us travelers back in the old days (the 1970's) Spain was almost as much different from the rich countries of Europe as were its Latin American cousins. All that changed with the demise of Generalissimo Franco and Spain's modernization and subsequent inclusion into the Eurozone. It's still a long fall from the glory days of the colonial Golden Age, but many countries have been and will go through that. So it's not as cheap as it was a few generations ago, but still cheaper than the northern European big boys, and indeed one of the liveliest of European countries these days. The nightlife only ends with daylight. Euro is the currency. Spanish is the language. Phone code is +34.

BARCELONA has a history that goes back to the Romans and the Carthaginians before them, the name possibly deriving from Hamilcar Barca, Hannibal's father. It was a camp for the Romans and gradually grew into a city, briefly the capital of Visigothic Spain, and then a victim of Arab conquest for some years before being liberated by Charlemagne's son Louis. It reached its peak of importance as part of the Crown of Aragon until union with Castile initiated a decline as second city to Madrid. Nowadays it may not be the country's capital of government, but it's definitely the capital of fun. It used to be the capital of industry.

Barcelona is well-connected to the rest of Europe by budget airlines, trains and Eurolines buses. This is the jumping-off point to Andorra, also, both of them members of the Catalonia club. The Gothic Quarter and Gaudi's Sagrada Familia church are top destinations in the city. Then there's Luis Doménechi Montaner's Music Palace, a UNESCO World Heritage site. Museums range from the maritime museum to the waxworks museum, the National Museum of Art of Catalonia, the Federico Marés Museum, the Museum of Modern Art and the Casa de Cervantes. There are also excellent beaches. Las Ramblas is ground zero for hostels, partying, and fun. Barcelona has one of the largest numbers of hostels in the world and quality is good.

www.barcelonaturisme.com/

Barcelona Central Garden Hostel, C/ Roger de Llúria 41 Spain; *http://barcelonacentralgarden.com/*, T:935006999, *barcelonagarden@gmail.com*; $35bed>, Kitchen:Y, B'fast:N, WiFi:Y, Pvt. room:Y, Locker:Y, Desk hr:9a>12m; **Note:** min. stay 2 Nights, free coffee & tea, laundry, no partying

Hostel One Paralelo, C/ Salvà, 62, Barcelona, Spain; *www.onehostel.com/*, T:934439885, *hosteloneparalelo@onehostel.com*; $27bed>, Kitchen:Y, B'fast:$, WiFi:Y, Pvt. room:N, Locker:Y, Desk hr:8a>10p; **Note:** free city tour, swimming pool, A/C, c.c. ok

AWA Barcelona Hostel Central, Pelai 11, buzz 'Casa', Barcelona, Spain; *www.awahostels.com/*, T:+33970440194, *reservations@awahostels.com*; $25bed>, Kitchen:Y, B'fast:N, WiFi:Y, Pvt. room:Y, Locker:Y, Desk hr:24/7; **Note:** a/c, laundry, good location

Sant Jordi Alberg, Roger de Lluria 40, piso 1° puerta 2ª, Barcelona, Spain; *www.santjordihostels.com,* **T:+34933023901,** *lluria@santjordi.org* $37bed>, Kitchen:Y, B'fast:N, WiFi:Y, Pvt. room:N, Locker:Y, Desk hr:24/7
Note: party hostel, laundry, TV, tea & coffee

Hostel One Sants, C/ Casteras 9, Barcelona, Spain; *www.onehostel.com/,* **T:933324192,** *hostelonesants@onehostel.com;* $21bed>, Kitchen:Y, B'fast:$, WiFi:Y, Pvt. room:N, Locker:Y, Desk hr:9a>12m;
Note: a/c, c.c. ok, bar, laundry, not in center but convenient to transport

Sant Jordi Sagrada Familia, C/ Freser, 5 Barcelona, Spain; *www.santjordihostels.com/,* **T:**934460517, *sagradafamilia@santjordi.org*; $30bed>, Kitchen:Y, B'fast:N, WiFi:Y, Pvt. room:Y, Locker:Y, Desk hr:24/7;
Note: party hostel, not central, laundry, elevator

Casa Gracia Barcelona Hostel, Passeig Gràcia, 116 Barcelona, Spain; *www.casagraciabcn.com/,* T:931874497, *info@casagraciabcn.com*; $37bed>, Kitchen:Y, B'fast:Y, WiFi:Y, Pvt. room:Y, Locker:Y, Desk hr:24/7;
Note: c.c. surcharge, laundry, elevator, partying discouraged

Sant Jordi Arago', Aragó 268 Pral. 1 Barcelona, Spain; *www.santjordihostels.com/,* **T:**932156743, *arago@santjordi.org*; $37bed>, Kitchen:Y, B'fast:N, WiFi:Y, Pvt. room:N, Locker:Y, Desk hr:9a>10p;
Note: laundry, café, left luggage, small hostel, near train, good location

Sant Jordi' Mambo Tango, C/ Poeta Cabanyes 23, Barcelona, Spain; *www.santjordihostels.com/,* T:**934425164,** *mambotango@santjordi.org*; $39bed>, Kitchen:Y, B'fast:Y, WiFi:Y, Pvt. room:N, Locker:Y, Desk hr:24/7;
Note: café & bar, laundry, left luggage, a/c

Itaca Hostel & Apts, Carrer de Ripoll, 21 Barcelona, Spain; *www.itacahostel.com/,* T:933019751, *pilimili@itacahostel.com*; $40bed>, Kitchen:Y, B'fast:$, WiFi:Y, Pvt. room:Y, Locker:N, Desk hr:24/7;
Note: min. stay 3N, deposit, surcharge late check-in, in Gothic Quarter

Alberguinn Y. H., Melcior de Palau 70-74, Entresuelo, Barcelona; *www.alberguinn.com/en/,* T:934905965, *alberguinn@alberguinn.com*; $31bed>,

Kitchen:Y, B'fast:Y, WiFi:Y, Pvt. room:N, Locker:Y, Desk hr:24/7;
Note: a/c, c.c. ok, close to Sants station, not central

Be Sound Hostel, C/ Nou de la Rambla 91, Barcelona, Spain;
http://behostels.com/sound, T:(0034)931850800, *sound@behostels.com*; $32bed>,
Kitchen:Y, B'fast:Y, WiFi:N, Pvt. room:N, Locker:Y, Desk hr:24/7;
Note: a/c, c.c. ok, laundry, rooftop drinks

Barcelona Pere Tarres Hostel, C/ de Numància, 149 Barcelona, Spain;
www.peretarres.org/alberg, T:934301606, *alberg@peretarres.org*; $34bed>,
Kitchen:Y, B'fast:Y, WiFi:Y, Pvt. room:Y, Locker:Y, Desk hr:24/7;
Note: a/c, terrace, laundry, bar, restaurant, metro close, not central

Sant Jordi' Diagonal, Diagonal 436, entresuelo, Barcelona, Spain;
www.santjordihostels.com/, **T:**932183997, *diagonal@santjordi.org*; $42bed>,
Kitchen:Y, B'fast:N, WiFi:Y, Pvt. room:Y, Locker:Y, Desk hr:9a>12m;
Note: tea & coffee, laundry, lounge, c.c. ok

Be Mar Hostel, C/ Sant Pau, 80 Barcelona, Spain;
http://barcelonamar.com/, T:933248530, *mar@behostels.com*; $29bed>,
Kitchen:Y, B'fast:Y, WiFi:Y, Pvt. room:N, Locker:Y, Desk hr:24/7;
Note: laundry, tour desk, city tour, a/c, c.c. surcharge

AWA Plaza Catalunya Hostel, Diputacio, 251, Tercero, Barcelona, Spain;
www.awahostels.com, T:+33970440194, *reservations@awahostels.com*; $31bed>,
Kitchen:Y, B'fast:N, WiFi:Y, Pvt. room:Y, Locker:N, Desk hr:24/7;
Note: a/c, lounge, tours, new

Be Dream Hostel, Avinguda Alfons XIII, 28, Barcelona, Spain;
http://behostels.com/dream/, T:933991420, *dream@behostels.com*; $26bed>,
Kitchen:Y, B'fast:Y, WiFi:Y, Pvt. room:Y, Locker:Y, Desk hr:24/7;
Note: next to beach, 30-day cancellation, lounge, laundry, c.c. ok

Barcelona Urbany Hostel, Av de la Meridiana, 97, Barcelona, Spain;
www.barcelonaurbany.com/, T:932458414; $34bed>,
Kitchen:Y, B'fast:Y, WiFi:Y, Pvt. room:Y, Locker:Y, Desk hr:24/7;
Note: tour desk, pool, a/c, gym, restaurant, bar, laundry, elevator, rooftop

Feetup Hostels-Garden House Barcelona, C/ Hedilla 58, Barcelona;
www.feetuphostels.com/, T:934272479; $28bed>,
Kitchen:Y, B'fast:$, WiFi:Y, Pvt. room:Y, Locker:N, Desk hr:24/7;
Note: non-party, far from center

Equity Point Centric, Passeig de Gràcia, 33, Barcelona, Spain;
www.equity-point.com/, T:932156538, *infocentric@equity-point.com*; $29bed>,
Kitchen:Y, B'fast:Y, WiFi:Y, Pvt. room:N, Locker:Y, Desk hr:24/7;
Note: bar, tour desk, laundry, elevator, terrace

Alternative Creative Youth Home, Ronda de la Universitat 17, Barca;
www.alternative-barcelona.com, T:635669021, *alvand@alberguest.com*; $36bed>,
Kitchen:Y, B'fast:N, WiFi:Y, Pvt. room:N, Locker:Y, Desk hr:24/7;
Note: ages 17-40, café, bike rent, a/c, c.c. ok, non-party, hard to find

Hello BCN Hostel, C/ de Lafont 8, Barcelona, Spain;
www.hellobcnhostel.com/, T:934428392, *info@hellobcnhostel.com*; $29bed>,
Kitchen:Y, B'fast:Y, WiFi:Y, Pvt. room:Y, Locker:Y, Desk hr:24/7;
Note: bar, wheelchair ok, luggage room, laundry, tour desk, a/c, c.c. ok

Downtown Paraiso Hostal, C/ de la Junta de Comerç, 13, Barcelona;
http://hostaldowntownbarcelona.com/, T:933026134; $47bed>,
Kitchen:Y, B'fast:N, WiFi:Y, Pvt. room:Y, Locker:Y, Desk hr:>10p;
Note: luggage room, c.c. ok, TV/DVD, some noise

Albareda Youth Hostel, Carrer d'Albareda 12, Barcelona, Spain;
www.albareda-youthhostel.com/ T: 934439466; $33bed>,
Kitchen:Y, B'fast:Y, WiFi:Y, Pvt. room:Y, Locker:Y, Desk hr:24/7;
Note: min. stay 2N, tour desk, a/c, c.c. ok, central, left luggage fee

Duo by Somnio Hostel, C/ del Rosselló 220, principal, Barcelona;
www.hostelduo.com, T:+34(0)932720977, *info@hostelduo.com*; $33bed>,
Kitchen:N, B'fast:$, WiFi:Y, Pvt. room:Y, Locker:Y, Desk hr:24/7;
Note: lift, luggage room, c.c. ok

Buba House, C/ d'Aragó, 239, Barcelona, Spain;
www.bubahouse.com/, T:935008318, *info@bubahouse.com*; $34bed>,

Kitchen:Y, B'fast:Y, WiFi:Y, Pvt. room:Y, Locker:Y, Desk hr:24/7;
Note: lift, luggge room, free tour, travel desk, central

The Kabul Hostel, Plaça Reial, 17, Barcelona, Spain;
www.kabul.es/, T:933185190, *info@kabul.es*; $26bed>,
Kitchen:N, B'fast:Y, WiFi:Y, Pvt. room:N, Locker:N, Desk hr:24/7;
Note: wheelchair ok, bar/club, free tour, travel desk, laundry, a/c

Lullaby Hostel, C/ Provença 318, E 1°, Barcelona, Spain;
www.lullabyhostels.com, T:934961874, *provenca@lullabyhostels.com*; $38bed>,
Kitchen:Y, B'fast:Y, WiFi:Y, Pvt. room:N, Locker:Y, Desk hr:24/7;
Note: café, lift, luggage room, laundry, a/c, c.c. ok, parties

Ona Barcelona, C/ del Consell de Cent, 413, Barcelona, Spain;
www.onabarcelona.com/, T:931858317, *info@onabarcelona.com*; $26bed>,
Kitchen:N, B'fast:N, WiFi:Y, Pvt. room:Y, Locker:Y, Desk hr:24/7;
Note: laundry, a/c, c.c. ok, non-tourist area

Mediterranean Hostel Barcelona, C/ de la Diputació, 335, Barcelona;
www.mediterraneanhostel.com, T:932440278, *info@mediterraneanhostel.com;*
$24bed>, Kitchen:Y, B'fast:N, WiFi:Y, Pvt. room:Y, Locker:Y, Desk hr:24/7;
Note: wheelchair ok, luggage room, laundry, a/c, c.c. ok

Hip Karma Hostel, Ronda de Sant Pere, 39, Barcelona, Spain;
www.hipkarmahostel.com, T:933021159, *hipkarmahostel@gmail.com*; $31bed>,
Kitchen:Y, B'fast:N, WiFi:Y, Pvt. room:N, Locker:Y, Desk hr:24/7;
Note: lift, bike rent, free tour, a/c, c.c. ok, hard to find, bunk curtains

A&A Arco YH, C/ de l'Arc de Santa Eulàlia, 1 Barcelona, Spain;
http://www.hostalarco.com/, T:934125468; $33bed>,
Kitchen:Y, B'fast:Y, WiFi:Y, Pvt. room:N, Locker:Y, Desk hr:24/7;
Note: wheelchairs OK, tour desk, laundry, c.c. OK, central

Somnio Hostel, C/ de la Diputació, 251, Barcelona, Spain;
www.somniohostels.com, T:932725308, *info@somniohostels.com*; $34bed>,
Kitchen:N, B'fast:$, WiFi:Y, Pvt. room:Y, Locker:Y, Desk hr:24/7;
Note: bar, lift, tour desk, c.c. ok, central

Albergue Palau, Albergue Palau, C/ Palau, 6, Barcelona, Spain; *www.bcnalberg.com,* T:934125080, *palau@bcnalberg.com;* $25bed>, Kitchen:Y, B'fast:Y, WiFi:Y, Pvt. room:Y, Locker:Y, Desk hr:24/7; **Note:** close to supermarket, c.c. ok, linen fee

Arian Y. H., Av. De la Mare de Déu de Montserrat 251, Barcelona; *www.arianyouthhostel.com/,* T:696504933, *info@arianyouthhostel.com;* $23bed>, Kitchen:Y, B'fast:N, WiFi:Y, Pvt. room:Y, Locker:Y, Desk hr:24/7; **Note:** tour desk, laundry, c.c. ok

BILBAO is the capital of Biscay province in Basque country, and is Spain's tenth largest city. Tourism is now a major industry in Bilbao, and its tourist attractions include the Guggenheim Museum. There is also the 14th C. Cathedral of Santiago in Gothic style, the 19th C. Plaza Nueva, San Antonio, Santos Juanes, and San Nicholas.

www2.bilbao.net/bilbaoturismo/index_ingles.htm

Ganbara Hostel, Calle Prim 11, Bilbao, Spain; *www.ganbarahostel.com,* T:944053930, *info@ganbarahostel.com;* $23bed>, Kitchen:Y, B'fast:Y, WiFi:Y, Pvt. room:N, Locker:Y, Desk hr:24/7; **Note:** bike rent, wheelchairs ok, luggage room, laundry, tour info, a/c

Surf Backpackers, Calle Ercilla 11 1° Izq, Vizkaia Bilbao, Spain; *www.surfbackpackers.com/,* T:+34(0)944754214, *surfbpsbilbao@gmail;* $33bed>, Kitchen:Y, B'fast:Y, WiFi:Y, Pvt. room:N, Locker:Y, Desk hr:lmtd; **Note:** café, bike rent, luggage room, a/c, c.c. OK, by Guggenheim, no sign

Botxo Galery/Y. H. Bilbao, Ave. de las Universidades, Bilbao, Spain; *http://botxogallery.com,* T:944134849, *info@botxogallery.com;* $22bed>, Kitchen:Y, B'fast:Y, WiFi:Y, Pvt. room:N, Locker:Y, Desk hr:lmtd; **Note:** wheelchairs ok, vending, forex, c.c. ok, a/c, triple bunks, central

CORDOBA lies 80 miles (130 km) northeast of Seville on the Guadalquivir River. It, too, was likely Carthaginian in origin. It became capital of Spain's Umayyad Muslims in 756 and grew rapidly thereafter. It was one of the most glorious cities in the world at the start of the previous millennium, full of palaces and mosques, before finally falling to the Christian Castilians in 1236. These days the entire old city is a UNESCO World Heritage site. Main attractions are the Roman Bridge and the Grand Mosque. The caliphs' main palace, the Alcazar, is now in ruins. Other classic buildings include monasteries and churches and the museums of fine art and archeology. Beside the old Moorish quarter there is also a Jewish quarter.

www.spain.info/en/ven/provincias/cordoba.html

Senses&Colours Anil Hostel, Calle de Barroso, 4, Cordoba, Spain; *www.sensesandcolours.com;* T:957491544, *maximo@sensesandcolours.com;* $18bed>, Kitchen:N, B'fast:N, WiFi:Y, Pvt. room:Y, Locker:N, Desk hr:24/7; **Note:** advise arrival time, linen & towel fee, wheelchair, a/c, terrace

Senses & Colours Seneca, Calle del Conde y Luque, 7, Cordoba, Spain; *www.sensesandcolours.com,* T:957473234, *seneca@sensesandcolours.com;* $18bed>, Kitchen:Y, B'fast:N, WiFi:Y, Pvt. room:Y, Locker:N, Desk hr:lmtd; **Note:** bar/lounge, tour desk, c.c. ok, linen/towel fee, Jewish quarter

GRANADA was a Jewish community before being selected as the capital of Moorish al-Andalus, some say as a vassal state to Castile, with the Reconquista in full swing after the fall of Seville in 1248. Nevertheless it was the last bastion of Moorish Spain, lasting until 1492, when the Moors were defeated, then along with the Jews forced to convert or leave. The oldest part of the city is in the northeast Albaicin quarter. The Alhambra "Palace City" was its heart. The Generalife was the palace of the Moorish sultans, and along with the Alhambra and Albaicin, is a UN World Heritage site. Other landmarks include the Cathedral of Granada and the palace of Charles V. The pomegranate ("Granada") is its symbol.

www.turgranada.es

El Granado, C/ Conde de Tendillas 7, Granada, Spain; *http://elgranado.com/,* T:958960259, *info@elgranado.com;* $29bed>, Kitchen:Y, B'fast:Y, WiFi:Y, Pvt. room:Y, Locker:Y, Desk hr:lmtd; **Note:** rooftop terrace, laundry, good location

Hostel Almora, Solanilla 7, Niguelas, Granada, Spain; *www.hostelalmora.com/en/*, T:677685800, *hostelalmora@gmail.com*; $18bed>, Kitchen:Y, B'fast:$, WiFi:Y, Pvt. room:Y, Locker:N, Desk hr:lmtd; **Note:** linen charge, contact for entry, village 50 min ride south of Granada

Oasis Backpacker's Hostel Granada, C/ del Correo Viejo, 3 Granada; *www.oasisgranada.com/*, T:958215848, *granada@hostelsoasis.com*; $25bed>, Kitchen:Y, B'fast:Y, WiFi:Y, Pvt. room:N, Locker:Y, Desk hr:24/7; **Note:** bar, city tour, laundry, c.c. ok, welcome drink, travel desk, in alley

Rambutan Guesthouse, Vereda de Enmedio, 5 Granada, Spain; *www.rambutangranada.com/*, T:958220766, *rambutangranada@hotmail.com*; $18bed>, Kitchen:Y, B'fast:Y, WiFi:Y, Pvt. room:Y, Locker:Y, Desk hr:24/7; **Note:** free bikes, great views, long walk from center

Funky Granada, C/ del Conde de las Infantas, 15 Granada, Spain; *http://funkygranada.weebly.com/*, T:958800058, *funky@altrernativeacc.com*; $22bed>, Kitchen:Y, B'fast:Y, WiFi:Y, Pvt. room:N, Locker:N, Desk hr:24/7; **Note:** bar, city tour, parking, c.c. ok, central

MADRID is the center of Spanish government and one of the financial capitals of Europe, as well as a center of tourism, but seems far from the Riviera ambience of which Barcelona is one of the capitals. Documented from the ninth century and the Arab era, Madrid rejoined Castile in 1085 and became capital in 1561, capital of an empire that spread around the globe. Today it's one of Europe's largest cities, and has many immigrants from the countries it once held sway over, giving it a lively cosmopolitan atmosphere. There are many nightlife and entertainment venues, but it's not the party center that Barcelona is, which may be good. El Prado is one of the best art museums in the world. Others are El Cason del Buen Retiro, Queen Sofia museum, the National Archeological Museum, the Thyssen-Bornemisza Museum, the Royal Academy of Fine Arts of the San Fernando Museum, and the Museum of the Americas. The *"Puerta del Sol"* is one of the busiest and most popular squares. Hostels are generally good.

www.esmadrid.com/en/portal.do

Hostel One Centro, C/ Carmen, 16 Madrid, Spain; *www.onehostel.com/*, T:915233192, *hostelonecentro@onehostel.com*; $28bed>, Kitchen:Y, B'fast:N, WiFi:Y, Pvt. room:N, Locker:Y, Desk hr:24/7; **Note:** city tour, laundry, a/c, café, maps, bike rental, left luggage

Hostel One Malasana, Manuela Malasaña 23 1º, Madrid; *www.onehostel.com/*, T:915915579, *hostelonemalasana@onehostel.com*; $22bed>, Kitchen:Y, B'fast:N, WiFi:Y, Pvt. room:Y, Locker:Y, Desk hr:24/7; **Note:** laundry, coffee & tea, city tour, c.c. ok, trendy Malasana 'hood

Way Hostel, C/Relatores, 17 Madrid, Spain; *www.wayhostel.com/*, T:914200583, *reservas@wayhostel.com*, $25bed>, Kitchen:Y, B'fast:Y, WiFi:Y, Pvt. room:N, Locker:Y, Desk hr:24/7; **Note:** city tour, travel desk, safe deposit, stairs

No Name City Hostel, C/Atocha, 45 Madrid, Spain; *www.nonamecityhostel.com/*, T:913692919, *info@nonamecityhostel.com* $22bed>, Kitchen:Y, B'fast:Y, WiFi:Y, Pvt. room:N, Locker:N, Desk hr:24/7 **Note:** lounge, city tour, laundry, cramped, few power outlets

Los Amigos Hostel, C/Arenal, 26 Madrid, Spain; *www.losamigoshostel.com/*, T:915592472, *reservassol@losamigoshostel.com*; $29bed>, Kitchen:Y, B'fast:Y, WiFi:Y, Pvt. room:N, Locker:Y, Desk hr:8a>12m; **Note**: a/c, c.c. ok, city tour, good location

Mad Hostel, C/ Cabeza, 24 Madrid, Spain; *www.madhostel.com/*, T:915064840, *info@madhostel.com*; $22bed>, Kitchen:Y, B'fast:Y, WiFi:Y, Pvt. room:N, Locker:Y, Desk hr:>9p; **Note:** laundry, a/c, couyrtyard, gym, roof terrace, small rooms, pool table

Equity Point Madrid, C/ de la Cruz, 5 Madrid, Spain; *www.equity-point.com/*, T:915323122, *infomadrid@equity-point.com*; $25bed>, Kitchen:N, B'fast:Y, WiFi:Y, Pvt. room:Y, Locker:N, Desk hr:24/7; **Note:** left luggage, elevator, bar, c.c. ok, big hostel, cozy rooms

The Living Roof Hostel Madrid, C/ Costanilla de San Vicente 4, Madrid; *www.thelivingroofhostel.com/*, T:915230578; $23bed>,

Kitchen:Y, B'fast:Y, WiFi:Y, Pvt. room:N, Locker:Y, Desk hr:24/7;
Note: walking tour, tapas tour, pub crawl, c.c. ok, travel desk

Barbieri Intl. Hostel, C/ Barbieri, 15, Madrid, Spain;
www.barbierihostel.com/, T:915310258, *booking@barbierihostel.com;* $24bed>,
Kitchen:Y, B'fast:Y, WiFi:Y, Pvt. room:Y, Locker:N, Desk hr:24/7;
Note: a/c, TV, lounge, c.c. ok

La Posada de Huertas Hostel, C/ Huertas (Centro), 21 Madrid, Spain;
www.posadadehuertas.com/, T:914295526, *info@posadadehuertas.com*; $25bed>,
Kitchen:Y, B'fast:Y, WiFi:Y, Pvt. room:N, Locker:Y, Desk hr:24/7;
Note: city tour, lounge, laundry, travel desk

MALAGA was under Arab dominance for some 800 years and that's almost appropriate, since it was first settled by their cousin forebear Phoenicians. Combined with the Romans and Spanish who have also ruled here, it all makes up for one of the more interesting histories in Europe. These days Malaga is better known as Europe's southernmost and warmest city. Tourist attractions include the Roman theatre and the Moorish fortress on Mount Gibralfaro. The cathedral was built in 1528 on the site of a mosque. The provincial museum of art includes works by Pablo Picasso, who was born here. The Moorish castle, Alcazaba, has been turned into a museum and garden. There are surprisingly few hostels and the quality is surprisingly irregular. Choose carefully and leave your options open.

www.malagaturismo.com/

Oasis Backpacker's Hostel Malaga, C/ San Telmo 14, Malaga, Spain;
http://hostelsoasis.com/, T:952005116; $19bed>,
Kitchen:Y, B'fast:Y, Wi-Fi:Y, Pvt. room:N, Locker:Y, Desk hr:lmtd;
Note: welcome drink, free city tour, rooftop bar, hard to find, central

Feel Malaga Hostel, Calle Vendeja, 25, Malaga, Spain;
www.feelmalagahostel.com, T:952222832; $27bed>,
Kitchen:Y, B'fast:Y, WiFi:Y, Pvt. room:Y, Locker:Y, Desk hr:lmtd;
Note: free popcorn, great location, hard to find, extra toilet paper!

Melting Pot, Av. del Pintor Joaquín Sorolla, 30 Malaga, Spain; *www.meltingpothostels.com/*, T:952600571, *malaga@meltingpothostels.com;* $24bed>, Kitchen:Y, B'fast:Y, WiFi:Y, Pvt. room:N, Locker:Y, Desk hr:24/7; **Note:** bar, laundry, on beach, not central, terrace, c.c. ok

Picasso's Corner, C/ San Juan de Letrán, 9 Malaga, Spain; *www.picassoscorner.hostel.com/*, T:952212287; $23bed>, Kitchen:Y, B'fast:Y, WiFi:Y, Pvt. room:N, Locker:N, Desk hr:24/7; **Note:** left luggage, c.c. ok, bar, laid-back vibe

Babia Hostel, Plaza de los Mártires, 6 Malaga, Spain; *www.babiahostel.com/*, T:952222730; $16bed>, Kitchen:Y, B'fast:Y, WiFi:Y, Pvt. room:Y, Locker:Y, Desk hr:lmtd; **Note:** bike rent, bar, restaurant

SAN SEBASTIAN is in Basque country, and only a stone's throw from France. Basques are descendants of the aboriginal inhabitants of the region with no known relation to any other peoples or language. If the tourist industry seems a bit fledgeling, there's a good reason. Until not so long ago secessionist activity was strong here. It seems like a surfers' town, and it's on my short list. For the cultured among you, the old town contains the Gothic church of San Vicente, the Baroque church of Santa Maria, and the former convent of San Telmo. Hostel quality is probably not up to big-city standards, but that can be nice, too. Choose carefully.

www.sansebastianspain.info/

Roger's House, C/ Juan de Bilbao 13-3°, San Sebastian, Spain; *www.hostel-rogers-house.com/*, T:943433856, *rogershouse@hotmail.es*; $40bed>, Kitchen:Y, B'fast:$, WiFi:Y, Pvt. room:N, Locker:Y, Desk hr:8a>12m; **Note:** rent bikes/boards, sports yes party no, café, cozy, old town, balcony

Pension Goiko, C/ del Puerto / Portu Kalea, 6 San Sebastián, Spain; *www.pensiongoiko.com/*, T:943431114, *pensiongoiko@hotmail.com*; $29bed>, Kitchen:Y, B'fast:Y, WiFi:Y, Pvt. room:Y, Locker:N, Desk hr:24/7; **Note:** old town, close to beach, c.c. OK, bike rent

Hospedaje Kati, C/ Fermin Calbeton Kalea, 21 San Sebastián, Spain; *www.hospedajekati.com/uk/index.htm*, T:943430487; $24bed>, Kitchen:N, B'fast:N, WiFi:Y, Pvt. room:N, Locker:N, Desk hr:24/7; **Note:** re-confirm by phone & advise arrival time, close to beach

Surf Backpackers, Narrica 23-2 dcha, San Sebastian, Spain; *www.surfbackpackers.com/*, T:943425511, *surfbackpackers@gmail.com*; $36bed>, Kitchen:Y, B'fast:N, WiFi:Y, Pvt. room:Y, Locker:Y, Desk hr:24/7; **Note:** good location

SEVILLE (Sevilla) is another part of Spain, older and with a much different history. The city is some 3000 years old and has one of Europe's largest "old towns" to prove it. This is where the Moors from North Africa ruled for over 500 years until the mid-13th century, and it still maintains much of that ambience to this day. This is also where trade from the New World flowed during Spain's Golden Age. The Alcazar and the Cathedral, both UNESCO World Heritage sites, are major tourist attractions. The Alcazar, begun by the Almohads in 1181, is the finest surviving example of Moorish architecture in the city. The cathedral was previously a mosque and the minaret still survives as bell tower. The adjacent Casa Lonja houses the General Archive of the Indies, a treasure trove of info on Spain's colonial period. The city museum houses paintings of the Sevilla School.

Five miles (8 km) northwest of the city are the ruins of the Roman city of Italica. There are numerous celebrations and festivals, of which the one during Holy Week (*Semana Santa*) is probably most important. The April Fair celebrates the Andalusian countryside. Sevilla is home to flamenco, and performances are frequent and lively. Hostel quality is high, and the tendency is toward partying, if not quite Barcelona. It's easy to get lost in the old quarter, especially at night, so carry your hostel's business card with you. You can always call a cab.

www.visitasevilla.es/

Traveler's Inn Seville, Plaza Alfalfa, 11, Seville, Spain; *www.travelersinnseville.com/*, T:954216724; $22bed>, Kitchen:Y, B'fast:Y, WiFi:Y, Pvt. room:Y, Locker:Y, Desk hr:24/7; **Note:** walking tour, tapas tour, pub crawl, a/c, c.c. ok, laundry

The Garden Backpacker, Calle Santiago, 19 Seville, Spain; *www.thegardenbackpacker.com/*, T:954223866, *reservas@thegardenbackpacker.com*; $21bed>, Kitchen:Y, B'fast:Y, Wi-Fi:Y, Pvt. room:N, Locker:Y, Desk hr:24/7; **Note:** bar, city tour, laundry, left luggage, free sangria, handicap access

Hostel One Seville Centro, C/ Angostillo 6, Seville, Spain; *www.onehostel.com/*, T:954221615, *hostelonesevilla@onehostel.com*; $13bed>, Kitchen:Y, B'fast:$, WiFi:Y, Pvt. room:Y, Locker:Y, Desk hr:8a>10p; **Note:** a/c, city tour, laundry, bike hire, good location

The Spot Central Hostel, Calle Adriano, 6 Seville, Spain; *www.thespotcentralhostel.com/*, T:955295837, *hi@thespotcentralhostel.com*; $20bed>, Kitchen:Y, B'fast:Y, WiFi:Y, Pvt. room:Y, Locker:Y, Desk hr:24/7; **Note:** free tour, sangria, cambio, c.c. ok, travel desk, terrace, clean, central

Hostel One Sevilla Alameda, C/ Jesús del Gran Poder 113, Seville; *www.hostelonesevilla.com/en/*, T:954909622; $21bed>, Kitchen:Y, B'fast:N, WiFi:Y, Pvt. room:Y, Locker:Y, Desk hr:8a>10p; **Note:** terrace, coffee & tea, c.c. surcharge, not central

Feetup Hostels-Samay Sevilla, Ave. de Menéndez Pelayo 13, Sevilla; *www.samayhostels.com/*, T:955100160, *sevilla@samayhostels.com*; $20bed>, Kitchen:Y, B'fast:$, WiFi:Y, Pvt. room:Y, Locker:N, Desk hr:24/7; **Note:** terrace, laundry, good location

Sevilla Inn Backpackers, Calle Mateos Gago, 15A, Seville, Spain; *http://sevillabackpackers.es/*, T:954219541, *booking@sevillabackpackers.es*; $23bed>, Kitchen:Y, B'fast:Y, WiFi:Y, Pvt. room:Y, Locker:Y, Desk hr:24/7; **Note:** bar, city tour, left luggage, terrace, free sangria, good location, paella

Oasis Backpacker's Hostel Sevilla, Calle de la Compañía 1, Sevilla; *www.oasissevilla.com/sevilla-hostel*, T:954293777, *sevilla@hostelsoasis.com*; $26bed>, Kitchen:Y, B'fast:Y, WiFi:Y, Pvt. room:Y, Locker:Y, Desk hr:24/7; **Note:** bar, coffee & tea, city tour, swimming pool, a/c, bike hire, need sign

The Living Roof, Calle Dos de Mayo, 16, Seville, Spain; *www.thelivingroofhostel.com/*, T:+34(0)954224371; $19bed>,

Kitchen:Y, B'fast:Y, WiFi:Y, Pvt. room:N, Locker:Y, Desk hr:24/7;
Note: terrace, c.c. ok, bar, travel desk, poor signage, only one bathroom

Sevilla Urbany Hostel, Maria Coronel 12, Seville, Spain;
www.sevillaurbany.com/, T:+34954227949; $13bed>,
Kitchen:Y, B'fast:Y, WiFi:Y, Pvt. room:N, Locker:Y, Desk hr:8a>11p;
Note: left luggage, tour desk, a/c, wheelchair ok, laundry

VALENCIA is Spain's third city and third region, with its own language and own history, spanning all the same major periods as the others—Roman, Visigoth, Arab, and Reconquest. El Cid briefly liberated it from the Moorish Almoravids late in the 11th century, but it did not become a full part of the Aragon crown until 1238, then united with the Castile of Ferdinand and Isabella in 1479. It is famous for its *paella* and its annual festival is the Fallas in March. The *fallas* are huge satirical monuments made of papier-mache and wax that are constructed over the course of a year. All except the best—on the eve of St. Joseph's feast day. Valencia has plenty of classic architecture and landscapes, some of which rate World Heritage status. Major landmarks include the Valenciana Cathedral and the Towers of the old city. Others are Lonja de la Seda (Silk Exchange), the Palacio de la Diputación, the Ayuntamiento (Town Hall), and the 18th C. Neoclassical Palacio de Justicia. Hostel quality seems generally good; unlike elsewhere, most are not chains.

www.turisvalencia.es/

Feet-up Hostels-Hilux Valencia, Cadirers 11 Pta 1 Valencia, Spain;
www.feetuphostels.com/, T:+34(0)963914691; $25bed>,
Kitchen:Y, B'fast:Y, WiFi:Y, Pvt. room:Y, Locker:Y, Desk hr:24/7;
Note: laundry, c.c. ok, central to all, no a/c

Home Backpackers, Plaza de Vicente Iborra, 46 Valencia, Spain;
www.homehostelsvalencia.com/, T:963913797; $20bed>,
Kitchen:Y, B'fast:N, WiFi:N, Pvt. room:N, Locker:Y, Desk hr:24/7;
Note: old town, free towel, rooftop terrace, big

Home Youth Hostel, C/ Lonja, 4 Valencia, Spain;
www.homeyouthhostel.com/, T:963916229; $25bed>,

Kitchen:Y, B'fast:N, WiFi:N, Pvt. room:Y, Locker:Y, Desk hr:24/7;
Note: laundry, bike hire, c.c. ok, a/c, close to central market

Russafa Youth Hostel, C/ Padre Perera, 5 Valencia, Spain;
www.russafayouthhostel.com/, T:963289460, *info@russafayouthhostel.com*;
$27bed>, Kitchen:N, B'fast:Y, WiFi:Y, Pvt. room:Y, Locker:Y, Desk hr:24/7;
Note: stairs, no left luggage, c.c. ok, min. stay 3 Nights in summer

Center Valencia Y. H., C/ Samaniego, 18 Valencia, Spain;
www.center-valencia.com/, T:963914915, *info@center-valencia.com/*; $16bed>,
Kitchen:Y, B'fast:Y, WiFi:Y, Pvt. room:N, Locker:Y, Desk hr:24/7;
Note: lift, bike hire, a/c, laundry, travel desk, wheelchair ok, central, quiet

24) Sweden

Swedes were first out of the gates of Scandinavia, first pushing southeast to the Crimea in the early years of the Common Era, then as Goths on a similar trajectory before dividing into *Ostro* and *Visi* and founding the first successor states to the Roman Empire in Italy, Spain, and elsewhere in the sixth and seventh centuries; and finally as proto-Viking "Varangian" *Rus*, who apparently founded the first Russian/Ukraine state. The modern state of Sweden finally began to emerge in the Middle Ages and by the 17th century, they had an empire to rival anyone in Europe. They lost all that, though, and today the emphasis is on quality of life, often regarded as the most egalitarian in the world. That comes with a price, of course.

Sweden ranks high in science and engineering, with many inventions and patents, and the economy includes both services and manufacturing, much of it high-tech and oriented toward export (Ericsson, anyone?). Alfred Nobel invented dynamite here and instituted the Nobel Prizes. Politics are heavily social-democratic internally and nonaligned and neutral externally. Sweden has managed to penetrate the English-speaking market for popular music and literature better than almost any other English-as-second-language country, with such popular music acts (all sung in English) as ABBA, Ace of Base, and Cardigans. Then there are the best-selling books of Stieg Larsson, not to mention the high art of playwright Strindberg or cineaste Bergman. Currency is the *krona*, phone code is +46, and the main language is Swedish, Finnish a second language.

www.visitsweden.com

GOTHENBURG is on Sweden's west coast about halfway between Copenhagen and Oslo and is the major seaport of the region. As such, it has always occupied a strategic position. The Dutch and Scots for a long time wielded a major influence here. There is also a major film festival and book fair. Nearby islands are reachable by ferryboat. The cathedral and the Kristine Church are notable landmarks and there are cultural, maritime, and natural history museums. There are many parks and an amusement park, also.

www.visitsweden.com/sweden/Regions--Cities/Gothenburg/

Kville Hotel B&B, Kvilletorget 24, Göteborg, Sweden;
www.kvillehotel.se/, T:0317441440, *info@kvillehotel.se*; $42bed>,
Kitchen:N, B'fast:Y, WiFi:Y, Pvt room:Y, Locker:N, Desk hr:lmtd;
Note: parking, laundry, a/c, c.c. ok, quiet neighborhood away from center

Slottskogens Y.H., Vegagatan 21, Göteborg, Sweden;
www.sov.nu/, T:031426520; $29bed>,
Kitchen:Y, B'fast:$, WiFi:Y, Pvt. room:Y, Locker:Y, Desk hr:lmtd;
Note: curtains on beds, laundry, luggage, forex

STOCKHOLM is the capital of Sweden and the largest city in all of Scandinavia. It was fully a part of European history by the mid-13th century as a regular port for the trade of the Hanseatic League, complete with many German-speakers, and was capital of the Swedish Empire. Today it is one of Europe's most desirable cities, clean and green and polished to a high sheen. Its location surrounded by open water keeps its temperatures moderate, despite its sixty-degree northern latitude. There is an old town. Landmarks include the Royal Palace; the Church of St. Nicolas; the German Church; the House of Lords; the Stock Exchange; Riddarholm Church; The House of Parliament and the National Bank. Summertime rocks, with nightlife everywhere. This far north closing time is… never.

www.visitstockholm.com/en/

City Backpackers Hostel, Upplandsgatan 2, Stockholm, Sweden;
www.citybackpackers.org/, T:468206920, *info@citybackpackers.se*; $34bed>,

Kitchen:Y, B'fast:$, WiFi:Y, Pvt. room:Y, Locker:Y, Desk hr:8a>2a;
Note: restaurant, luggage room, linen charge, bike rent, c.c. ok

Langholmen Hostel STF/HI, Långholmsmuren 20, Stockholm;
www.langholmen.com, T:087208507, *hotel@langholmen.com;* $37bed>,
Kitchen:N, B'fast:$, WiFi:Y, Pvt. room:Y, Locker:N, Desk hr:24/7;
Note: member discount, bar/café, luggage ok, wheelchair ok, parking

The Red Boat Malaren, Södermälarstrand Kajplats 10, Stockholm;
www.theredboat.se/, T:086444385, *info@theredboat.se;* $39bed>,
Kitchen:N, B'fast:$, WiFi:Y, Pvt. room:Y, Locker:N, Desk hr:8a>1a;
Note: resto/bar, luggage ok, c.c. ok, on boat in water, hard to see at night

Jumbo Stay, STF/Him Jumbovägen 4, Stockholm Arlanda Airport;
www.hihostels.com/, T:+46(0)859360400, *booking@jumbostay.com;* $59bed>,
Kitchen:N, B'fast:$, WiFi:Y, Pvt. room:Y, Locker:N, Desk hr:24/7;
Note: resto/bar/café, luggage ok, a/c, cc ok, arpt. pickup, converted 747

STF/HI Fridhemsplan, S:t Eriksgatan 20, Stockholm, Sweden;
www.hihostels.com./, T:+4686538800, *info@fridhemsplan.se;* $41bed>,
Kitchen:Y, B'fast:$, WiFi:Y, Pvt. room:Y, Locker:Y, Desk hr:24/7;
Note: parking, laundry, a/c, c.c. ok, non-HI surcharge, clean, central

Skanstulls Vandrarrhem, Ringvägen 135, Stockholm, Sweden;
www.skanstulls.se/, T:086430204, *kontakt@skanstulls.se/;* $35bed>,
Kitchen:Y, B'fast:N, WiFi:Y, Pvt room:Y, Locker:Y, Desk hr:3p>8p;
Note: max. stay 7N, luggage ok, bikes, c.c. ok, no basement windows

Crafoord Place, Hälsobrunnsgatan 10, Stockholm, Sweden;
www.crafoordplace.se/, T:08337133, *info@crafoordplace.se;* $33bed>,
Kitchen:Y, B'fast:N, WiFi:Y, Pvt room:N, Locker:Y, Desk hr:10a>6p;
Note: 2N min., lift, parking, free tour, a/c, c.c. ok, travel desk, coffee/tea

Best Hostel Old Town, Skeppsbron 22, Stockholm, Sweden;
www.besthostel.se/en, T:+46(8)4119545, *contact@besthostel.se;* $32bed>,
Kitchen:Y, B'fast:Y, WiFi:Y, Pvt. room:Y, Locker:N, Desk hr:lmtd;
Note: luggage room, laundry, c.c. ok, coffee & tea, central

2kronor Hostel- Vasastan, Surbrunnsgatan 44, Stockholm, SE; *www.2kronor.se/*, T:+468229230, *info@2kronor.se*; $36bed>, Kitchen:Y, B'fast:N, WiFi:Y, Pvt. room:Y, Locker:Y, Desk hr:9a>6p; **Note:** laundry, luggage room, central, midday lockout

Interhostel, Kammakargatan 46, Stockholm, Sweden; *http://interhostel.se/*, T:084112311, *info@interhostel.se*; $33bed>, Kitchen:Y, B'fast:N, WiFi:Y, Pvt. room:Y, Locker:Y, Desk hr:>2a; **Note:** linen fee, laundry, luggage OK, c.c. ok, no window in dorm

Best Hostel City, Luntmakargatan 14, Stockholm, Sweden; *www.besthostel.se/sv*, T:08218418, *city@besthostel.se*; $39bed>, Kitchen:Y, B'fast:Y, WiFi:Y, Pvt. room:Y, Locker:N, Desk hr:lmtd; **Note:** luggage room, lift, laundry, c.c. ok, central

UPPSALA is only forty minutes from Stockholm by train, so if the big city is booked up (no joke), then consider staying here. It's less than a half hour to Stockholm's airport. It was an early religious center, with a pre-Christian town 3mi/5km north. Besides the Gothic cathedral, there is a castle that is now the governor's residence, the botanic garden and house of Carolus Linnaeus, and the Victoria Museum, with Egyptian antiquities. It's a university town, too.

www.destinationuppsala.se

Vandrarheim Centralstation, Bangårdsgatan 13, Uppsala, Sweden; *www.hotellcentralstation.se/*, T:0761858485, *info@hotellcentralstation.se*; $30bed>, Kitchen:Y, B'fast:$, WiFi:Y, Pvt. room:Y, Locker:N, Desk hr:24/7; **Note:** luggage ok, bikes, c.c. ok, $11 linen fee, no windows, central

Vandrarhem Uppsala-Kungsangstorg, Kungsängstorg 6, Uppsala; *www.vandrarhemuppsala.se*, T:0761858485, *info@vandrarhemuppsala.se*; $30bed>, Kitchen:Y, B'fast:$, WiFi:Y, Pvt. room:Y, Locker:N, Desk hr:lmtd; **Note:** central, staff scarce, linen $5, towel $5, c.c. ok

STF/HI Uppsala/Vandrarhem, Kvarntorgsgatan 3, Uppsala; *www.hihostels.com/*, T:4618242008, *kvarntorget@uppsalavandrarhem.se*; $33bed>, Kitchen:Y, B'fast:$, WiFi:Y, Pvt. room:Y, Locker:Y, Desk hr:8a>7p; **Note:** towel + linen=$12, luggage ok, resto/bar, a/c, no windows, far

25) Switzerland

Switzerland is much like Belgium to the west in its role as a transition state between northern and southern Europe. Here, though, the north and the German language predominate, and the Alps provide a common identity. Switzerland is famous for its direct democracy and its historical neutrality, its banking secrecy and its watchmaking industry. It is also a high-tech economy with one of the highest incomes per capita in the world. That makes it expensive of course. The mountains are the predominant theme for recreation, with skiing in winter, hiking and biking in summer. The Swiss franc is currency; the phone code is +41; languages are German, French, Italian, and Romansch.

www.infoplease.com/ipa/A0108012.html

BASEL is located where Switzerland meets France and Germany (with suburbs in those countries). It sits on the Rhine and is Switzerland's only cargo port. As such it is also a rail hub and industrial center, yet still with plenty of culture and sights to see. It has a very interesting Protestant Carnival, which starts on the Monday after Ash Wednesday at 4 a.m. and lasts exactly seventy-two hours, consuming the town with festivities. Landmarks include the Protestant Münster church; the late Gothic Rathaus, or town hall; the Church of St. Martin; and the former 14th-century Franciscan church, now housing the historical museum. It is a mainly German-speaking city.

www.basel.ch/en/

YMCA Hostel Basel, Gempenstrasse 64, CH-4008 Basel; *www.ymcahostelbasel.ch,* T:0613617309, *info@ymcahostelbasel.ch*; $34bed>, Kitchen:Y, B'fast:$, WiFi:Y, Pvt. room:Y, Locker:Y, Desk hr:7a>11p; **Note:** noon lockout, central, lift, wheelchair ok, parking, laundry, c.c. ok

Basel Back Pack, Dornacherstrasse 192, Basel, Switzerland; *http://baselbackpack.com,* T:+41(0)6133300, *info@baselbackpack.com*; $35bed>, Kitchen:Y, B'fast:$, WiFi:Y, Pvt. room:Y, Locker:Y, Desk hr:8a>8p; **Note:** café/resto/bar, bike rent, noon lockout, lift, forex, c.c. ok, central

Youth Hostel Basel, *St. Alban*-Kirchrain 10, *Basel;* *www.youthhostel.ch/,* T:+41612720572, *basel@youthhostel.ch*; $46bed>, Kitchen:Y, B'fast:Y, WiFi:Y, Pvt. room:Y, Locker:N, Desk hr:24/7; **Note:** YHA chg, resto/bar, wheelchair ok, luggage ok, c.c. ok, veg food

BERN'S entire medieval center has been named a UNESCO world heritage site and is the most traditional in all of Switzerland. This includes the *Zytglogge* clock tower and the *Nydegbrukke* bear pit. You don't see that every day. There's also the Gothic cathedral, the City Hall, the Nydegg Church, the Federal Palace (Bundeshaus) and the Cage Tower. Einstein lived here, too.

www.bern.ch/en/welcome

Berne Backpackers Hotel Glocke, Rathausgasse 75, Berne, Switzerland; *www.bernbackpackers.ch/,* T:0313113771, *info@bernbackpackers.ch*; $38bed>, Kitchen:Y, B'fast:N, WiFi:Y, Pvt. room:Y, Locker:Y, Desk hr:8a>10p; **Note:** c.c. ok, laundry, noisy club, central, few power sockets, tea/coffee

INTERLAKEN is located between lakes, as the name indicates, and lies in the central German-speaking part of the country. Its role as a foundation stone of the Swiss tourism industry goes back to its origins in the early 1800's, when good transportation links could shuttle passengers in to view the fabled landscapes already well known in the artworld. Despite two world wars, they still come for the mountain air and outdoor activities.

www.myswitzerland.com/en/interlaken.html

Backpackers Villa Sonnenhof, Alpenstrasse 16, Interlaken, Switzerland; *www.villa.ch/*, T:0338267171, *mail@villa.ch*; $32bed>, Kitchen:Y, B'fast:Y, WiFi:Y, Pvt. room:Y, Locker:Y, Desk hr:lmtd; **Note:** left luggage, laundry, parking, forex, c.c. ok, mountain views

Balmer's Herberge, Hauptstrasse 23, Matten b. Interlaken, Switzerland; *www.balmers.com/*, T:0338221961, *mail@balmers.com*; $32bed>, Kitchen:Y, B'fast:Y, WiFi:Y, Pvt. room:Y, Locker:Y, Desk hr:24/7; **Note:** resto/bar, club, forex, laundry, luggage ok, c.c. ok, noon lockout

Funny Farm Backpackers, Hauptstrasse 36, Interlaken, Switzerland; *www.funny-farm.ch/*, T:0338281281, *info@funny-farm.ch*; $22bed>, Kitchen:N, B'fast:$, WiFi:Y, Pvt. room:Y, Locker:N, Desk hr:24/7; **Note:** bar, restaurant, club, forex, parking, laundry, travel desk, c.c. ok

Lazy Falken Backpacker, Spielmatte 8, Unterseen, Switzerland; *www.lazyfalken.ch/*, T:0338223043, *info@lazyfalken.ch*; $34bed>, Kitchen:Y, B'fast:Y, WiFi:Y, Pvt. room:Y, Locker:Y, Desk hr:lmtd; **Note:** bar, café parking, laundry, left luggage, forex, c.c. ok

Happy Inn Lodge, Rosenstrasse 17, Interlaken, Switzerland; *www.brasserie17.ch/ws/br/en/happyinn/hostel/*, T:0338223225, $27bed>, Kitchen:Y, B'fast:$, WiFi:Y, Pvt. room:Y, Locker:Y, Desk hr:6a>1a; **Note:** bar, parking left luggage, c.c. ok

LUCERNE is a small city in the German-speaking central part of Switzerland, and a mainstay of the local tourist destinations. It is on a lake and within sight of Switzerland's highest mountains. Traditional and alternative cultures coexist and many festivals are held in the warm season. The Spreuerbrücke, Lucerne's oldest bridge, is roofed and decorated with some fifty-six paintings, scenes from the Dance of Death, something of a Middle Age precursor to 1970's Grateful Dead imagery, I guess. The old town contains the old town hall and historical museum, Am Rhyn House, St. Peter's Chapel, the Hofkirche and the Mariahilf Church, Bertel Thorvaldsen's "Lion of Lucerne" monument, and the Glacier Garden. There are steamer services on the lake and cableways to ski resorts.

www.luzern.ch/en

Backpackers Lucerne, Alpenquai 42, Lucerne, Switzerland; *www.backpackerslucerne.ch,* T:0413600420, *info@backpackerslucerne.ch;* $35bed>, Kitchen:Y, B'fast:N, WiFi:Y, Pvt. room:N, Locker:Y, Desk hr:lmtd; **Note:** laundry, fore, c.c. ok, left luggage, on lake not central

Lion Lodge Lucerne, Zürichstrasse 57, Lucerne, Switzerland; *www.lionlodge.ch/,* T:0414100144, *info@lionlodge.ch*; $35bed>, Kitchen:Y, B'fast:N, WiFi:Y, Pvt. room:Y, Locker:Y, Desk hr:8a>10p; **Note:** restaurant, parking, laundry, no lift

Youth Hostel Luzern, Sedelstrasse 12, Lucerne, Switzerland; *www.youthhostel.ch,* T:0414208800, *luzern@youthhostel.ch*; $35bed>, Kitchen:N, B'fast:Y, WiFi:Y, Pvt. room:N, Locker:Y, Desk hr:7a>12m; **Note:** parking, c.c. OK, not central, skyhlights

ZERMATT is where you go to climb the Matterhorn. It's also a car-free zone, internal combustion, that is; electric or nothing, way cool. Tourism is almost the only business.

www.zermatt.com/

Zermatt Youth Hostel, "Winkelmatten" Staldenweg 5, *Zermatt; www.youthhostel.ch,* T:+41279672320, *zermatt@youthhostel.ch*; $56bed>, Kitchen:N, B'fast:Y, WiFi:Y, Pvt. room:Y, Locker:Y, Desk hr:>10p; **Note:** dinner inc, resto/bar, tour desk, laundry, c.c. ok, kiosk, terrace, view

Matterhorn Hostel, Schluhmattstrasse 32, Zermatt, Switzerland; *www.matterhornhostel.com,* T:0279681919, *info@matterhornhostel.com*; $39bed>, Kitchen:Y, B'fast:$, WiFi:Y, Pvt. room:Y, Locker:Y, Desk hr:8a>9p; **Note:** resto/bar, TV/DVD, central, luggage room, c.c. ok

ZURICH was once an outpost of the Celtic Helvetii and Romans before falling under the influence of the Franks and Alemanni, and before joining the Swiss Confederation, a group united in opposition to the Austrian Habsburgs. Its location at the crossroads of trade routes put it at the center of political and economic events on the cutting-edge of history. Soon it became a manufacturing powerhouse, and a bastion of Protestantism, democratic reform,

AND finance. Culture followed, and Zurich became the center of the Dada art movement. But it was not all inspired. Its banks' role in laundering Hitler's money became known in the 1990's and it repaid millions to Jewish families plundered.

Today it is the largest and wealthiest city in Switzerland. It's beautiful, too, but expensive. It has major film, art, and music festivals, including the dance-and-techno-oriented "Street Parade," which attracts a million people. Raemistrasse, just east of the city centre, is known as the city's "art mile." Notable museums include the Swiss National Museum, and the Museum of Fine Arts. Historic architecture is centered in the old town, including the 8th C. Grossmunster, 13th C. St. Peter's Church, and the Fraumunster, with windows by Marc Chagall. With its increasing ethnic diversity, it is one of Europe's liveliest of modern cities.

www.zuerich.com/

Youth Hostel Zurich, Mutschellenstrasse 114, Zurich, Switzerland;
www.youthhostel.ch, T:0433997800, *zuerich@youthhostel.ch;* \$46bed>,
Kitchen:Y, B'fast:Y, WiFi:N, Pvt. room:Y, Locker:Y, Desk hr:24/7;
Note: non-members \$6 extra, luggage, laundry, bar, parking, distant, large

26) Wales

Wales is the other country comprising the United Kingdom—besides England, Scotland and Northern Ireland—and is arguably the most traditional of the lot. It is more or less defined by its non-Anglo roots, and is the remnant of a once-large area of original non-Germanic peoples in post-Roman Britain. You can hear radio programs in Celtic here; you'll be hard pressed to find that in Scotland. The Romans ruled for several hundred years, but Anglo-Saxons made little impact until after the Norman Conquest in 1066. Shortly thereafter the Cardiff Castle was built and English settlers began trickling in. Wales was soon absorbed into England's affairs, and made official partner with an Act of Union in 1536. Since then, Wales was been most closely identified with coal mining, an activity in sharp decline these days. Now a post-industrial economy, tourism in Wales is on the rise. Blaenavon, an early coal-mining and ironworks center, is now a UNESCO site. Pound sterling is currency, phone code is +44, and the languages are English and Welsh.

www.walestouristsonline.co.uk/

CARDIFF is the largest city and commercial center of Wales, and formerly the largest coal port in the world. Services and tourism are big today, with Cardiff Castle being one of the major attractions. There are also other castles, hence its claim to have more castles than anywhere else in the world. Other historic buildings include Llandaff Cathedral and the medieval parish church of St. John. Also worth visitng are the Welsh National Museum and Gallery; Techniquest, an interactive science museum; and the Museum of Welsh Life, at St. Fagan's Castle, 4.5 miles (7 km) west of the city centre. There are ruins of burial chambers near Cardiff that pre-date Stonehenge. With its status as a port, Cardiff is ethnically diverse. There is a huge free festival called Cardiff Big Weekend held every summer. There is an active nightlife. Hostels are generally good here, divided between party and non-party ones.

www.visitcardiff.com/

Riverhouse B'packers, 59 Fitzhamon Embankment, Cardiff, S. Wales;
www.riverhousebackpackers.com/; T:0292039 9810; $29bed>,
Kitchen:Y, B'fast:Y, WiFi:Y, Pvt. room:Y, Locker:Y, Desk hr:24/7;
Note: towel fee, laundry, "not a party hostel," central, cats

Nomad Hostel, 11-15 Howard Grdns, Roath, Cardiff, S. Glamorgan;
www.nomadcardiff.co.uk/, T:02920256826, info@nomadcardiff.co.uk; $19bed>,
Kitchen:Y, B'fast:Y, WiFi:Y, Pvt. room:Y, Locker:Y, Desk hr:24/7;
Note: bar, laundry, towel fee, left luggage fee, central

NosDa Studio Hostel, 53-59 Despenser Street, Riverside, Cardiff;
http://nosda.co.uk/, T:02920378866, *info@nosda.co.uk*; $32bed>, Kitchen:Y,
B'fast:Y, WiFi:Y, Pvt. room:Y, Locker:Y, Desk hr:24/7;
Note: bar, c.c. ok, gym, min. 2N wknds, parking, live music, loud at times

Bunkhouse Hostel, 94 Saint Mary St, S. Glamorgan, Wales UK;
www.bunkhousecardiff.co.uk/, T:02920228587, info@bunkhousecardiff.co.uk;
$24bed>, Kitchen:N, B'fast:Y, WiFi:N, Pvt. room:N, Locker:Y, Desk hr:24/7;
Note: club, central, loud on wknds, right on pub strip

YHA Cardiff, 2 Wedal Road, Roath Park, Cardiff UK;
www.yha.org.uk/, T:08453719311, *cardiff@yha.org.uk;* $25bed>,
Kitchen:Y, B'fast:$, WiFi:$, Pvt. room:N, Locker:Y, Desk hr:7a>11p;
Note: temporary membership fee, distant

About the Author

Hardie Karges has traveled to 150 countries and is the author of "Hypertravel: 100 Countries in 2 years," published in 2012. "Backpackers and Flashpackers in Western Europe" is his second book.